Buz

Jane Holt

Buzzoodle Buzz Marketing

Ron McDaniel

www.buzzoodle.com

Published by Buzzoodle Publishing

Information about Buzzoodle Publishing can be found on the Buzzoodle Web site. Buzzoodle Publishing publishes innovative books and training materials to help small businesses succeed at sales and marketing.

McDaniel, Ronald E.
Buzzoodle Buzz Marketing

ISBN : 1-4196-4758-X
Library of Congress Control Number : 2006908005

To order additional copies, please contact us.
BookSurge, LLC
www.booksurge.com
1-866-308-6235
orders@booksurge.com

Buzzoodle Buzz Marketing

Table of Contents

Medium Buzzoodle Buzz Challenges

"The success of an organization is the responsibility of every member." – Ron McDaniel

We live in a global economy where every organization is competing with every other organization on the planet. It is no longer an issue of managers, labor, and owners. Today's issue is how your organization will survive against a much bigger pool of competitors. If you feel perfectly safe, you don't see how quickly things are changing.

Buzzoodle Buzz Marketing is a book about teamwork and the cultivation of a workforce that not only does a remarkable job, but also understands that everyone in the organization is responsible for creating a bit of buzz to help gain visibility, market share, and success. Today's communication tools make it possible for even the most quiet of team members to be a powerful marketing force.

As a group your organization will succeed or fail. Do not leave all of the buzz and word-of-mouth responsibilities in the hands of a few people. Word of mouth is the most powerful force in motivating people to purchase, and the more positive word of mouth each team member creates, the more resources the organization will have for its growth and success.

In an average five minutes per day per person your organization will experience heightened visibility and faster growth. It will transform some employees into industry experts and build stronger relationships with clients. With little or no cost, your organization can become talked about all over the world.

Buzzoodle Buzz Marketing tells you how.

Praise for Buzzoodle Buzz Marketing

So often today you read about creating buzz or word of mouth, but rarely do you get real guidance. Ron McDaniel gives you specific actionable steps that can be followed by anyone in your workforce to start creating buzz to grow your business – today!"

Anita Campbell, Editor
Small Business Trends – www.Smallbiztrends.com

"*Buzzoodle Buzz Marketing* is THE handbook for word-of-mouth marketing! The Buzz Challenges offer easy ways that anyone can use to create AMAZING buzz for their company or their life. If you need more paying customers, and who doesn't need more paying customers, this is a book you must get today!"

Phil Gerbyshak, M.I.G. Co-pilot and author of
10 Ways to Make It Great! – makeitgreat.typepad.com

"Whether you are an individual, a small business, a nonprofit, or a huge corporation, *Buzzoodle Buzz Marketing* has valuable practical advice that can benefit you greatly. If you want to find the right employment, obtain money and volunteers for a nonprofit, or increase your company's sales, this book can provide you with methods you probably never thought of. Ron is an extraordinarily creative Web-oriented entrepreneur whose ideas are grounded in reality."

Dr. William L. Shanklin, Visiting Professor of Marketing, University of Akron; author, consultant to business and corporate board member

"If you're tired of no one knowing about your top-notch products or services, get *Buzzoodle Buzz Marketing*. It's filled with fun activities to engage your staff in creating big-time buzz about your company without having to spend a small fortune."

Jill Konrath, Author, *Selling to Big Companies*
Chief Sales Officer, www.SellingtoBigCompanies.com

"Finally, a practical guide that helps EVERY employee easily market his or her company through their ordinary day-to-day actions."

Ted Demopoulos, Consultant and Speaker,
Demopoulos Associates - Coauthor, *Blogging for Business*

"The information contained in *Buzzoodle Buzz Marketing* will help any company set itself apart from the competition and grow. In today's competitive and volatile marketplace, we need every edge possible, and buzz marketing is a key piece to gaining that edge. This book will guide the way to success in buzz marketing and create a true team atmosphere within an organization. Great things will happen!"

David M. Ciccarelli, President
The Sirak Financial Companies

"*Buzzoodle* has been an invaluable tool for our school district. It has helped us get to the good news out to our stakeholders in a quick and easy twenty-first century way."

Dr. Marc Crail, Superintendent, Kent City Schools, Ohio

"Every business that struggles with how to market its products and services should read this book. Ron has created a process to allow everyone in the company, no matter the position, to be a buzz marketer. A must read for all business owners who want to grow their business by creating positive buzz. This is a powerful book!"

Ron Finklestein, Small Business Success Expert, author of *Celebrating Success! Fourteen Ways to Create a Successful Company* and *The Platinum Rule for Small Business Mastery*

"*Buzzoodle Buzz Marketing* is compact and concise. Not only does it do a great job of reminding us of many existing buzz creating techniques, it includes many new ideas, twists and enhancements in a fun, easy read."

Guy Shirk, President/CEO, Bottom Line Strategies

"*Buzzoodle Buzz Marketing* organizes the power of positive attitude into a simple straight forward process that can be used anywhere as long as you have positive people."

Terry Webb, Director of Residential Life
Binghamton University, Binghamton, New York

"Accountants have a very similar profile to that of computer engineers. We saw the same reluctance to promote our firm by many of our best staff. When we stopped asking them to "sell" and simply asked them to adopt the *Buzzoodle* philosophy and share stories of how we were able to help companies reduce their taxes legally and safely, they did not hesitate. We are really creating some wonderful Buzz around town now and our most recent revenue gains are quite remarkable."

David Gaino, Chairman, Moore Stephens Apple

"*Buzzoodle Buzz Marketing* is loaded with simple yet tremendously effective tools for creating the word-of-mouth buzz that can transform any business, from the mom-and-pop operation to the Fortune 500."

Joe Heuer, author of *Business Daffynitions: Humor from the Workplace* and *The Idiot-Proof Guide to Customer Loyalty*

"Who's your marketing machine? Your team is...."

"Buzz" is a marketing powerhouse that builds your business, but you have to do it right. Ron McDaniel teaches you "Buzz Marketing" techniques... how to coach your team and hold them accountable to effectively market your business to huge revenues. In today's modern marketing world... this is a must read!

Ralph Berge, Business Coach and President
Action International of the North Coast

Preface

When I began writing this book, I actually began writing two books. One was to be a workbook for a workforce and other advocates to use to help them create buzz. The other book was to be for executives on building a buzz strategy.

The final book, which you now hold in your hands, is a combination of the two. For people in the workforce to be inspired to create buzz, they need to know why it is important and how it will benefit them. For executives it is important that they participate in buzz challenges and do the same things they are asking employees to do.

Eventually I will write a more detailed book about the Psychology of Buzz. It will be full of facts and figures and research. It will convince the most skeptical of chief marketing officers that word of mouth and buzz are the most important aspects of their effort.

For now, I will rely on your good common sense. If you believe that positive buzz and good word of mouth are important to your organization, this book is for you.

Who Benefits from this Book?

These techniques have been used in 2006 by schools to pass levies, businesses to dominate their industries, nonprofits to increase funding, and religious organizations to grow membership. Any organization that can benefit from higher visibility will benefit from this book.

Business Owners: Read this book and identify your buzz strategy and guidelines. This book will help you prepare to launch a buzz campaign with your workforce.

Employees: This book is an opportunity for you to become an expert in your field, to help your organization succeed, and to become even more essential to your organization. Good buzz creators have great job security.

Salespeople: Read this book and find new ways to generate leads, and even more importantly, find new ways to get other people to generate leads for you.

Marketing Specialists: Use this book to guide your word-of-mouth marketing strategies with clients. Buzzoodle Buzz Marketing is a great addition to any engagement.

Nonprofits: Often associations and nonprofits have a very limited budget for marketing. This book in the hands of each advocate will help the organization succeed without an increase in spending.

Politicians: *Buzzoodle Buzz Marketing* is a proven method of increasing visibility and building the kinds of personal connections that make a big difference in elections.

Business Leaders: The more enthusiastic team you have, the more buzz you can create. Visionary leaders that implement team buzz marketing with this book will find many benefits that will move them ahead of the competition and enhance the organization's relationships with customers and the public.

If you and your organization can benefit from higher visibility and positive word of mouth, I guarantee that this book is a great return on your investment and time. Nothing else I have ever seen can have more of an impact than mobilizing a passionate group of advocates and giving them tools to reach millions of people.

Let's get going....

Introduction

You as Buzz Marketer

Have you ever tried to go through an entire day never mentioning a brand, a person, a book, a movie, a restaurant, a product, or an organization? Try it; it is hard. The fact is, we are all buzz marketers and many of us don't even realize it.

Buzz is when lots of people start talking about something, writing about something, e-mailing, blogging, and passing along messages in any format possible. The more messages that are passed, and passed again, the more intense the buzz.

What may surprise you is that people who are not directly involved in sales and marketing are often more comfortable talking about other people and businesses and not about where they work.

There is a very good chance that you talk more about restaurants, movies, and books than you do about your workplace. When people speak well about something, they are helping the person or company they are talking about. Shouldn't the entire team try to create some buzz and enjoy working in a more successful organization as well?

Imagine working for an organization with 100 employees. Let's say seven of them are in sales, and every day they try to close sales to help the organization grow. If they succeed, everyone benefits. If they fail, some of the non-sales staff may lose their jobs. Everyone's fate is in the hands of the few salespeople.

Now imagine that every employee in the organization spends a few minutes each day creating a little bit of buzz. How does that change the equation?

First, many more inquiries come in to the sales staff instead of the staff having to go out and get them. Instead of convincing the client to buy, the sales staff is just taking the order. The client was already sold by the buzz.

Also consider a salesperson calling a prospective client. The caller will meet with more success when the prospect says, "I have heard about you..."

This book is designed to be a guide for team members in an organization to create buzz on behalf of the organization that pays their wage. Not everyone will participate, and some may even resent the request, but a vast majority of people understand that working for a more successful organization with more resources is preferred over one that is less successful. In today's marketplace, buzz can be the difference between being at the top of an industry and being invisible in an industry.

By encouraging staff to create buzz, your organization has a low-cost, high-impact way to stand out and grow. With every team member committed to the success of the organization and creating buzz, everyone will prosper.

To all my family for supporting me along the journey.

To Neo, Alexandra, and Maya for being my inspiration and joy.

To Kandace, whom I wish I knew better.

Part One

Before Creating Buzz

Welcome Aboard

There is a good chance that this book is in your hands because it was given to you by an employer who is striving to grow and be more successful by creating more advocates for the organization, especially through team buzz. This book has been written to provide you with an overview of why this strategy is important and to provide you with fifty-seven Buzzoodle Buzz Challenges that you can follow to help create buzz every day.

Before creating any buzz, be sure to read the first sections to understand how buzz works, what to do, and what to avoid to be more successful. Also check with your employer for additional guidelines and recommendations for creating buzz. The guidelines in this book are just general and your organization may have special rules for what you can say.

Once you have read though the book once, skim it frequently and write in it. Each Buzzoodle Buzz Challenge has a page facing it with some key questions and plenty of space to take notes and record buzz attempts.

Organizations that want to create the maximum buzz must encourage people to keep their book out and handy and share their efforts and successes among the staff. Specific goals should be set for creating buzz. By setting goals and writing them down, then measuring how many buzz marketing challenges someone has completed, you are much more likely to be successful.

Important: First Do No Harm

Keep in mind that complaining about where you work may just seem like blowing off steam, but if you say the wrong thing to the wrong person, it could lead to widespread bad buzz and hurt you and your coworkers. Always bring up complaints or problems with the appropriate person in your organization and do not express the negative feelings publicly.

Even frequently complaining to a spouse could be hurting the success of where you work. When you consider that your spouse talks with others and may repeat your negative buzz, this could be heard by the wrong person.

Buzzoodle Negative Buzz Tip

I have frequently had people ask me if we were hiring. They then launched into complaining about their current employer. As a business owner, I would never employ someone who complains openly about a workplace. If someone is asking about a job, I know the person is not fully happy.

Even if you are not happy at work, keep it professional and positive or you may just be hurting yourself.

What is Buzzoodle Buzz Marketing?

Buzzoodle Buzz Marketing is a fundamental belief that advocates actively engaged in creating regular word of mouth for a high-quality product or organization will eventually build up substantial positive buzz. This buzz will help the organization dominate the industry if the competition does not adopt a buzz strategy as well.

Buzzoodle is unique in Buzz Marketing because its focus is on making your workforce into a stronger advocacy base. With the whole team creating regular, positive word-of-mouth messages, your organization's visibility will soar.

Buzzoodle History in the Blink of an Eye

Buzzoodle came about because of my own frustration. Buzzoodle was conceived in 2005 after a few sleepless nights. Our business was doing well but we wanted to grow faster. We wanted to give bigger raises, improve benefits, get nicer offices, and make more money. I held a staff meeting and made a simple request. I asked the non-sales staff to talk about us more. I asked them, specifically, to create more buzz about us.

While these employees were excellent at what they did, they were uncomfortable with the request. One said he did not know anyone who needed our products because he only hung out with losers. I pointed out that even losers have successful relatives, and the debate went on.

Finally one of the programmers looked me dead in the eye and uttered the sentence that would keep me up at night. "It is not my job."

This person was an excellent employee and a great person. He just felt that it was not part of his job description. At that time, he was making considerably more than I and I knew it was a serious issue. I felt that all employees must be contributing to the success of the organization in every way possible. I knew there was a disconnect between the attitudes and expectations of the employees and the success of the business, and I needed to find a solution. I needed to move them from being employees to being part of a winning team dedicated to group success.

Many sleepless nights later, Buzzoodle was born. It began as a software system that would challenge and track buzz efforts by team members. While the software functioned well, it did not prove easy enough to encourage people to keep using it. Finally we made the commitment to books, training courses, and products that could easily be accessible to anyone. We knew we needed something that would sit on someone's desk and beg them to make a difference in the success of the organization. This book is the result of that need.

Creating Buzz Today

Today buzz is easier to create than at any other time in history. Anyone can communicate a message to a neighbor, a city, a region, or the world through the Internet. The Buzzoodle Buzz Challenges are simple activities that any team member can do to create buzz. They have been written with the busy staff person in mind and most take only a few minutes. Many challenges take no special skill and not all of them involve technology, so all people can find challenges they feel comfortable with.

Any given challenge may create huge buzz or disappear in a whisper. **The key today is to get your message out in lots of ways to lots of people in a word-of-mouth fashion.** This book is about how to do that. People pay more attention to word of mouth and they have learned to filter out the advertisements that bombard them.

By asking each person to create and broadcast word-of-mouth messages, an organization is creating a stream of natural, sincere messages that get noticed. The end goal is that every member of the organization contributes to the success of the organization not only through an employee's specific role, but also by being an advocate for the business.

Everyone benefits from creating buzz.

The Employee as Advocate

It is obvious that organizations benefit from employees creating buzz. If a person shows up as an employee, that person is showing up for a paycheck. If an employee shows up as an advocate, that employee is showing up to be a winner and part of a successful team. How does this benefit the advocate?

- The organization has more success, which provides the team with more security.

- Individuals who contribute more to an organization's success could expect more opportunities and rewards in the future.

- A work atmosphere that encourages buzz is frequently a more open and fun environment.

- Creating buzz gives team members an opportunity to learn about and use new technologies and improve communication skills.

- Team members who become active buzz creators can become respected as industry experts over time and may get invited to speak and write.

- Team members who are good buzz creators will have other opportunities from within an organization and from outside as well.

- Good buzz creators tend to know more people and can accomplish more in life via their extensive network.

Remember it is a win-win situation. Sell yourself, sell your expertise, and sell your employer. Having a company full of industry experts would be a great thing.

An Eye for Success

To begin creating buzz successfully, you first must understand the power of success. Your organization is probably full of success stories that you are unaware of. If you are going to create buzz, you have to know what these successes are. You will want to start collecting these success stories to give everyone more things to talk about. You will also want to start telling people within the organization about these successes.

Your organization should formalize how these stories get collected and disseminated throughout the organization. Here are some suggested avenues to use to get the word out internally.

Newsletter
Publish a newsletter that is distributed on a regular basis. Offer incentives for the best buzz story about the organization.

Group E-mail
Send out regularly scheduled e-mails of success stories and examples of buzz to an employee e-mail list. For smaller groups you can let all of the group e-mail to the list. For larger groups, you may want to have someone moderate the list.

Bulletin Board
Post examples and challenges on bulletin boards in break areas.

Intranet
An intranet is a great place to post detailed stories that people can read and use to create their own buzz. Testimonials can also be collected in the same area and used by everyone.

Blog
Blogs are powerful buzz marketing tools. Consider making a public blog where the organization posts all of the success stories. Make sure team members are periodically reminded where it is and how submit to articles whenever a success is achieved.

Internet Message Boards
Internet message boards are similar to blogs but allow for more threaded conversations. If people have questions and discussions around your success stories, a message board may be a good format.

Staff Meetings

I hope you are already doing this, but be sure someone is addressing successful buzz efforts in staff meetings. Public recognition and appreciation will lead to more buzz.

Paycheck Stuffer

Quick notes in the paycheck about buzz efforts can be a regular reminder. Maybe the monthly winner of "Best Buzz Award" can be highlighted.

Luncheon

Bigger meetings, usually involving food, are a good way to let everyone know about new successes of the organization and the group's commitment to buzzing. Consider a quarterly luncheon that focuses on buzz and success.

Speech – Live or Video

In a bigger organization, having an executive give a speech either live or via a video feed can boost morale and reaffirm the organization's commitment to buzz. The executive can give examples of buzz created by other people and how he or she creates buzz. Everyone needs to know that there is 100% participation.

Podcast Messages

Podcasts are audio files that people can subscribe to. A podcast message that is regularly recorded by a senior staff person can be a great way to create buzz and keep the staff informed of the buzz efforts. The team can then load the comments on a music player and listen to them while traveling or listen to them at the computer.

The biggest key for each person in the organization is to watch for success stories and to let the right person know about them for easy broadcasting to all advocates. Make it easy for everyone to create buzz by letting everyone know what is happening that is buzz-worthy.

Part Two

Why Word of Mouth?

Word of mouth is something people just do. Pay attention to yourself each day as you talk about a variety of brands and products. Why did you do free advertising for those brands? Why would you become an uncompensated salesperson for a company that does not even know you exist?

To begin with, people like to give advice and feel like an expert. A big part of how they are perceived is based on their ability to make high-quality recommendations that help the people they know.

Take this book for example. If it helps you grow your business or create buzz, you very well might refer it to a friend or business acquaintance. You will not refer it because you care about me and my hungry children; you will do it because you found it valuable and by referring it, you will be creating value for someone else at no cost to you. You are unlikely to refer it to someone who is not involved in business because the value of the referral would be lower for the person. The person simply does not need the knowledge in this book.

If you tell someone about a valuable resource or product and the person uses it and also finds it valuable, you will be credited with the value it provides. You will become a better resource and your opinion in the future will have more value. If the referral is extremely valuable, it could even result in some sort of reward, commission, acknowledgement, job offer, or other bonus, but that rarely is the catalyst to do word of mouth.

People like to provide quick, easy value to others. The key to getting started with creating buzz for your organization is to fully understand the value you provide and share the success stories that will demonstrate your organization's value. How does the organization add to the value and experiences of a person's life?

You can increase the buzz you create for where you work by paying attention each time you recommend something or discuss a brand, company, or product. What made you talk about it? What made the topic come up in conversation and why was it interesting to both of you? Is the other person likely to repeat it to others? You can learn a lot about word of mouth and creating a buzz just by listening to your own conversations. Is there a way to adapt your company's success stories to what you are already talking about?

What you will find as you pay attention to the things you recommend is that they have remarkable qualities that make them stand out from the crowd. Do the recommendations have a great benefit or a great design that makes them worth talking about? Do you have a feeling that the benefit is something interesting to the person you are making the recommendation to?

One-to-one recommendations will be based on a perceived need or interest of the individual. It can also happen with a strong friendship that enables sharing of stories where people can discuss benefits they received. People creating buzz may also just feel strongly about the benefit they received and create buzz online, broadcasting it to anyone in the world who is interested in particular information. Depending on the influence some people have, a few minutes of their time may create unbelievable buzz.

Your organization has success stories. It provides benefits to its customers. It must to survive. To thrive, an organization must create remarkable benefits that make it stand out from others. This could be as simple as remarkable customer service. It must make you stand out from the ordinary. Every action by every person in the organization contributes to its atmosphere and has the potential to make the organization remarkable.

How Word of Mouth has Changed

Word of mouth has changed drastically in the past few years. Not what is being said, but the vehicles that carry it. Word of mouth was once an important but local affair. Now with technology, news about your organization – good and bad – spreads around the globe in seconds and one person can be the gateway to thousands of people knowing your story, with or without your permission.

You can develop the same reach by using technology to develop friendships, influence, and expertise. When I started Buzzoodle, I started blogging regularly for the first time. Blogging is just one type of technology that enables you to publish short articles frequently and allows people to read your writing. Over time you develop an audience that comes back regularly. The key is to keep at it and have something interesting to say.

Within a few months of starting my blog, people at some of the top companies in the world were calling and writing to me as an expert in the field. I'd spent very little money and just made a point of writing a few minutes each night, and the world came knocking at the door.

Around this same time, I e-mailed a popular author and blogger named Seth Godin, sending him a quick note telling him what our company was doing. He gave us a lukewarm blog post and a link to the Buzzoodle site. A few days later we had people signed up in fourteen countries and got hundreds of members and thousands of Web site visitors.

Word of mouth has changed and anyone you meet may have influence and access to far more people than you think. Consider if you are in a restaurant and talking loudly with your spouse about problems at work. People sitting at the next table hear you complaining. They may blog about it as an example of what not to do. They may even mention the company name if they hear it. People around the world will read it and spread it as an example of what not to do.

The consequences to the company may include developing an image as a bad place to work, having unhappy employees, or being a place that is in trouble. The consequences to the individual who was complaining could be losing the job. If a small comment triggers a firestorm of bad buzz, you can be sure that many organizations will look into the issue.

A recent example of this (2006) is when an Internet repairman called to get help with something while on a repair. He waited on a support call with the company he works for so long that he dozed off on the couch at the house he was doing the repair. The home owner had set up a camera and caught it all on tape. Last I heard, hundreds of thousands of people had downloaded the video, the company had made a public apology, and the installer was "no longer with the company." Always assume someone is watching or listening.

The Internet is important for global and local buzz. In many cases, locally focused companies think they are immune to the Internet. Local people talking, local press coverage, and local advertising is all they need, they believe.

Local buzz is very powerful if you have a community-based business or organization. A restaurant or church will probably not care if people in Hong Kong are hearing about them. But do not be fooled by this. The Internet has global reach and makes for powerful local community building.

The Internet is where many local groups form to keep in touch, share experiences and post their opinions. Even a local business can develop a robust online buzz that will create positive impressions and more visibility to the right people.

Non-salespeople are Better Buzz Marketers

Why are non-salespeople better Buzz Marketers? They are better at creating buzz because they are not selling.

Organizations today are moving toward a model where they utilize great word of mouth and buzz marketing, and the salespeople are simply the closers and the order takers. The salespeople are the people who understand the process that someone will need to follow to make the purchase or commitment. Because of the buzz, the emotional decision to purchase has already taken place in advance.

Gone are the days of cold calls, super bowl ads, SPAM, and mass direct mail. Sure you can still give them a try, but without word of mouth you are just creating noise.

Creating buzz and word of mouth with your team, customers, and people in your outer circles will create a larger interest in your organization than any slick marketing campaign. People listen to non-salespeople for the same reason they are more likely to read a handwritten note. It is authentic, unpolished, and honest.

Most marketing people won't tell you about something that is less than perfect. Non-sales employees might tell you how, behind the scenes, it is much more work than it seems and how they have to take extra steps to keep customers happy. From marketers, this just seems like a selling tactic, but from people who work the extra hours, you get a feeling of appreciation for their effort and you care about their success. Their unpolished sincerity comes through.

How Does Your Work Culture Help Buzz?

A work culture of buzz is created by people's behavior, attitude and professionalism. It also thrives in an environment where people can have some fun and express themselves. Word of mouth is at best guided by marketing, but is really an organic movement of people excited to participate. Any organization can cultivate an environment that makes buzz part of its culture and it can start at any level of the organization.

People who enjoy work are more likely to buzz about it. One way to create a more buzzable environment is to share successes and stories that are buzz-worthy about the organization and its people.

All new hires should understand what makes the organization special. They should be given examples, tools and training for creating more buzz. Guidelines must be reviewed with them to be sure they understand the goals and the restrictions. Be sure to ask all new hires why they are excited to work there. Try to keep them excited and help them make a difference through their job and the buzz they create.

The entire team should be encouraged to share buzz stories and successes where they have created buzz with other team members. Recognition of buzz creation and group activities around creating buzz are very important. Competitions can make it more fun. Also helping someone become a recognized expert in a field will help the company and the individual. Team members will want to be a part of the personal and group success.

Once your work culture fully embraces buzz as a part of the daily activity, the organization will become more successful, it will become a more enjoyable place to work, and every member of the organization will benefit from the higher visibility and tangible buzz being created.

Buzzoodle Tip

To get a jump-start on creating buzz for your organization, organize a buzz party. This is a voluntary, after-work event where everyone stays over or works through lunch and creates some buzz. Some people may make blog posts, some may organize events, send letters, do podcasts, update the Web site or any of the fifty-seven Buzz Marketing challenges in this book.

If you get the group together and get people focused on buzz as a group on a regular basis, you will find you have a stronger team dedicated to the success of the organization.

Part Three

Start Buzzing

Now that you are ready to start creating buzz, there are some basic things everyone needs to do or keep in mind. This list is especially important for larger organizations that should prepare a strategic plan and guidelines for teams creating buzz. These lists are good places to begin formalizing those guidelines.

Seven Things to Do

- Check with your buzz organizer to get guidelines for creating buzz.

- Always spell-check and review for grammar mistakes in anything you write before publicizing.

- Set a goal to create buzz every day. Many of the Buzzoodle Buzz Challenges take only a few minutes.

- Review your customer service. Make the customer's day unusually exceptional and they will buzz about you.

- Monitor the buzz you create each day for other brands and products. Why do you talk about them and how could you make your own organization more buzz-worthy?

- Report any problems or negative buzz you encounter to the appropriate person. Help stop bad buzz before it starts.

- Report buzz and organizational success stories to the appropriate person.

Nine Things Not To Do

Just as there are many things that are universally important to do, there is also a list of things that you should avoid doing. Unless, of course, your organization explicitly says they want controversy and possibly negative buzz.

- Do not state personal views in a buzz effort when they might conflict with the organization's stated views or cause unwanted controversy.

- Do not disclose information that may be a trade secret, private in nature, or damaging to the organization.

- Do not mention client names unless you have permission from the client and your organization.

- Do not fake buzz. Be sincere.

- Do not use unethical buzz tactics, such as posing as someone else.

- Do not create bad buzz. Address issues with your organization's management.

- Do not engage in an online argument that may lead to bad buzz. If a situation has the potential to get out of hand, refer it to the organization's specified expert.

- Do not disregard a complaint or concern from a customer. Address it and create a fan for the organization and for you.

- Do not attack your competitors. Take the high road and focus on standing out.

Part Four

Buzzoodle Buzz Challenges

What is a Buzzoodle Buzz Challenge?

Buzzoodle Buzz Challenges are different ways you can create buzz for a product or organization. Individual challenges may or may not create buzz in a particular instance, but the idea behind them is that if a group of people are buzzing on a regular basis for a high-quality product or service, buzz will spread.

Not all Buzz Challenges are appropriate for every product, service or team member. Take time to highlight those challenges you would be interested in doing and you believe will be effective for your organization. This book has been designed so that you can write in it. Take notes and record when you use a challenge, so that you can monitor your progress and success.

Keep this book on your desk or someplace where you can see it, as a reminder to create buzz. Share your Buzzoodle Buzz Marketing book with other team members and discuss your experiences with each other so that you get a feel for what other people are experiencing as well.

The following section contains the best challenges for getting everyone involved in creating buzz. Some are very quick and should be done frequently, like keeping your contacts fresh. Others take time, effort, and money, and might be done only by executive-level employees, board members, and business owners. If you have a question about a buzz challenge, talk to your designated buzz organizer.

Buzzoodle Buzz Challenges do not have to be done in any specific order nor are they all necessary. In fact, it is better to master a few you are successful with than to try to do all of them. Find the ones you are comfortable with, give them a try, and measure the results. Try to step out of your comfort zone and do some that take more effort. This could lead to you discovering a new interest or skill, as well as create some buzz for the organization.

The challenges have been organized into three groups: Simple, Medium and Advanced difficulty. There is no specific order within the difficulty groups. Which ones work for you will depend on you, your organization, product, and service.

These challenges give you an overview of activities you can do to create buzz. If you need more information on a specific challenge you can visit **www.Buzzoodle.com** or do an Internet search to find out more on the topic.

Buzzoodle Challenge Ratings

While most challenges have been selected because anyone can do them, some have also been included that may require approval for expenses and require longer time commitments. If you are unsure of your organization's policies on doing longer challenges or challenges that have an associated fee, check with your buzz organizer.

We have also rated challenges based on our best guess for difficulty. This will vary based on each individual's skills; what is difficult to some may be easy for others. Effectiveness will also vary based on the message more than the technology and buzz technique.

Each challenge will have the following ratings defined to help you identify buzz challenges that are within your scope.

Difficulty: *Simple, Medium, or Advanced*

The overall difficulty rating helps buzz creators know how easily they can do the challenge for the first time. This will vary based on your experience and technical savvy, but it gives you a ballpark estimate.

Cost: *Minimal, Costly, or Varies*

Every challenge has a cost, even if it is the cost of one minute of your time. Minimal cost means there should be no unexpected cost besides something small like postage. Varies means that the challenge may or may not cost money depending on how you do it. For example, if a challenge says to invite people over for dinner, it could cost you money for the food or you could organize a potluck dinner.

Time: *Quick, Medium, or Ongoing*

Many challenges are designed to take no more than a few minutes. Those that take significant planning will be marked as medium. Ongoing means that an ongoing commitment is required, such as blogging regularly.

Technology: *None, Simple, or Advanced*

Simple technology is for technology that many people use daily, such as e-mail, cell phones and other common tech communications tools. Advanced technology is for those technologies that will take some studying and effort to learn. No challenges require advanced programming or engineering skills.

Success Secrets for Your Buzz Challenges

Here are some basic principles that will help you be more successful with buzz challenges. These success secrets are centered on building quality relationships and being generous. Keep these in mind when buzzing and you will be building good will and standing out from the crowd.

- Talk less than half the time. A good listener will always stand out more than someone who dominates a conversation and does not give others a chance to speak.

- Build a personal network even if you do not need it. You may not be in sales and you may not need to know lots of people, but start behaving like a network is essential to your job and success. A strong network will always pay dividends eventually.

- Don't be afraid of Link Love. Link to other people's Web sites, blogs, and other online resources and they will often link back to you.

- Don't hold back. Connect with people when you have the chance. Say hi and smile more. Don't wait for someone else to break the ice.

- Give generously. No, don't give away your money. Give people value by making introductions with people they will benefit knowing. Give people information they will like reading. Give value and knowledge without worrying about how you are going to make money that day.

Buzz depends on people talking to other people. It starts with you. Build good will and great relationships and creating buzz will be a much easier task.

Buzzoodle Buzz Challenges

Check off preferred challenges.

Buzzoodle Buzz Challenges –Difficulty: Simple

E-mail an Old Friend or Acquaintance   —
Contact a Stale Connection   —
E-mail Extended Family   —
Call Someone You Have Never Talked To   —
Send a Congratulations Call or Note   —
Send a Surprise Letter   —
Send an Any Day Card   —
Mail a News Clipping   —
Engage in Social Networking   —
Create an Online Directory   —
Build a Squidoo Expert Lens   —
Tag Your Web site or Blog   —
Write a Blog/Message Board Comment   —
Join/Participate in an Online Group   —
Talk to a New Person in Person   —
Contact a Reporter or Writer   —
Contact an Old Employer/Employee   —
Do Customer Follow-Up   —
Call/E-mail a Person You Respect   —
Send Mini Announcements   —
Digg your Web site   —
Have Some Flickr Fun   —
Create a Personal Success E-mail List   —
Try: Did you know? Trivia   —
Use Instant Messaging   —
Send a Text Message   —
E-mail a Useful Link to Someone   —
Give Testimonials   —
Celebrate Success   —

Buzzoodle Buzz Challenges – Difficulty: Medium

Write a Blog —
Have a "Get to Know You" Meal —
Host a Dinner Party —
Arrange Networking Lunch —
Publish an Article —
Meet More Neighbors —
Send a Press Release —
Give a Speech —
Volunteer —
Conduct an Online Interview/Podcast —
Conduct a Survey —
Get Involved with Local Government —
Hold an Open House —
Interview a Leader —
Explore Youtube.com —
Meet business neighbors —
Create an eNewsletter or Newsletter —
Produce an eBook —
Nominate Organization —
Challenge a coworker to a Buzz-Off —

Buzzoodle Buzz Challenges – Difficulty: Advanced

Produce a Podcast Show —
Host a Seminar or Training Session —
Have an Unexpected Booth —
Organize a Group —
Become a Board Member —
Conduct Focus Group/Roundtable —
Conduct a Contest with Customers —
Organize a Charitable Event —

Challenge Notes:

Buzzoodle Buzz Challenge #1

E-mail an Old Friend or Acquaintance

Difficulty..........................Simple
Time...............................Quick
Cost...............................Minimal
Technology Required......Simple

Send an e-mail to an old friend or acquaintance. You might know the person from school, an old job, or the person may be a client you have not talked to in a while. Share what is new in your life and the positive things that are going on in your job.

Mention it has been a while since you have talked and you would like to find out what is new with that person as well. If you are not sure, ask about where the person is working now. If the person is in your area, you might want to suggest meeting for lunch.

One of the keys here is to leverage your prior relationship to tell a positive story about where you work without spoiling the conversation by blatantly selling the company or being impersonal. Depending on your relationship, you might mention something about your job, such as an open position or a specific need.

I recently heard a story about someone getting a call from an old college acquaintance. It had been many years since they'd talked and the person called and asked for $10,000. The person telling the story said, "I felt sorry for him. How many people did he call before me?"

Build your network before you need it and keep in touch. It is good for you and it is good for creating buzz for your organization.

Buzzoodle Buzz Notes

List some people with whom you need to catch up.

How many e-mails have you sent to date for this challenge?

From whom have you gotten favorable responses?

Who has this challenge helped you get to know better?

Has your organization gotten good buzz from this challenge?

Buzzoodle Buzz Challenge #2

Contact a Stale Connection

Difficulty.........................Simple
Time.............................Quick
Cost.............................Minimal
Technology Required......Simple

In today's busy world, we get contacted by many people and it is impossible to keep every connection fresh. If you get a lot of e-mails, your older e-mails are a goldmine of possible buzz.

Look through your e-mails or call journal for contacts that are about three months old, choose a couple, and reconnect with them. It could be by e-mail or by phone, but refresh the connection.

It is fairly easy to do. Just say you have been very busy but you wanted to follow up with them because you value getting to know them. Ask them some questions about what has changed in the last three months with them and let them know at least one success story from where you work if the opportunity presents itself.

If you are uncomfortable talking about work with people, start by asking them about where they work. It is easy to piggyback on their comments and talk about your organization.

If every person in your organization connected with three people like this each month, consider the ramifications. Large organizations could be generating many leads from this warm-up technique, and even if not sales leads, a certain percentage of these people are going to be impressed you checked back in and they will talk about you. This is a super easy and super important challenge that anyone with e-mail should do.

Buzzoodle Buzz Notes

List some people you have not contacted in a while with whom you need to catch up.

How many contacts have you made to date for this challenge?

From whom have you gotten favorable responses?

Additional notes for actual benefits the organization has received due to your efforts on this challenge.

Buzzoodle Buzz Challenge #3

E-mail Extended Family

Difficulty..........................Simple
Time.............................Quick
Cost.............................Minimal
Technology Required....Simple

Take this buzz challenge and get to know one of those extended family members. If you do not have family, choose someone who is related to someone you are close to.

E-mail the extended family member and describe how your job is going and ask about other family members. Keep it personal and light. Mention a success story and ask some questions to find out how the person's career is going. If you do not know the person well, ask more questions. If you really do not know the person, you may have to introduce yourself and explain how you are related.

You would be amazed how many people have a wide variety of family members who do not have any idea what they do. Don't explain your job; simply share a success story about how you helped someone. The person will probably understand such a story better than the technical details about your job.

Offer to get together or have a phone conversation in the near future. Keep in mind that the goal is to build your network and create a little buzz, so describe why you love working where you work, in a natural way, of course.

Be sure to impart any news that might interest them, such as a job opening or new people you have met.

Buzzoodle Buzz Notes

List some extended family with whom you need to reacquaint yourself.

How many e-mails have you sent to date for this challenge?

From whom have you gotten favorable responses?

With which people has this challenge improved your relationship?

Additional notes for actual benefits the organization has received due to your efforts on this challenge.

Buzzoodle Buzz Challenge #4

Call Someone You Have Never Talked To

Difficulty..........................Simple
Time..............................Quick
Cost..............................Minimal
Technology Required.......None

E-mail has become very prevalent. Chances are you have a lot of connections with people who you have never talked to. It could be because you met via e-mail, or it may be a customer or prospect you have exchanged mail with but never had the opportunity to get to know.

Give one of these people a call and find out a little more about the person. This is an easy one. Just call and say, "Hi. I thought it was time to actually talk in person." Have some questions prepared in case the conversation does not take off.

Be sure to ask about the person's job and what the person does. Work positive stories into the conversation about your organization. If appropriate, set up a time to get together or follow up.

If you cannot think of someone who you have never talked to, catch up with someone you have not talked to in months.

If you would like to increase the difficulty a bit, try calling someone you have read about in a newspaper or magazine. Introduce yourself, say what you do, and then find out a bit more about the person and what the person does. Let the person know what you liked about what you read. Have some questions prepared so that you are just not calling to talk about yourself, which is a very unbuzzworthy thing to do.

Don't be surprised when people seem a bit confused. People rarely call to be nice and express appreciation for what someone is doing. The person you talk to will be waiting for the sales pitch.

Buzzoodle Buzz Notes

List some people you have not met but would like to talk to.

How many calls have you made to date for this challenge?

From whom have you gotten favorable responses?

What has been the result of your best conversation?

Additional notes for actual benefits the organization has received due to your efforts on this challenge.

Buzzoodle Buzz Challenge #5

Congratulations Call or Note

> Difficulty.........................Simple
> Time...............................Quick
> Cost...............................Minimal
> Technology Required.......None

Create a little buzz by congratulating someone for succeeding. If you read something in the paper, on the Web, in a magazine, or if you hear about it in person, let the person know you know and offer your congratulations. Doing this with a phone call is best because it will give you a chance to say a bit about what you do as part of the conversation.

What you have heard or read will give you clues to ask good questions. How did you get in the paper? How did you achieve that success so easily? What are you going to do next and is there anything I can do to help you?

If you do not want to call the person, send a congratulatory note and a copy of what you read. Make sure you handwrite the note so that it has a personal touch and is more likely to get noticed.

This challenge not only works with news items, but with family-related items as well. If you know someone has a child or spouse in sports, theater, college, or some other activity, pay attention to the successes of the child or spouse and send a congratulatory note. People notice when you notice their family.

There is no end to the connections you can make to people via this challenge. Some of our best relationships have come from this kind of connection. Several have resulted in mutually beneficial partnerships over time. Any opportunity to express interest in someone is an opportunity you should seize.

Buzzoodle Buzz Notes

List some kinds of people you would like to reach and the kinds of places there will be news about them.

How many news sources have you read for this challenge?

Whom have you contacted?

From whom have you gotten favorable responses?

Additional notes for actual benefits the organization has received due to your efforts on this challenge.

Buzzoodle Buzz Challenge #6

Send a Surprise Letter

Difficulty......................Simple
Time............................Quick
Cost...........................Minimal
Technology Required....None

Sometimes a random handwritten letter can have a fantastic effect. If someone takes the time to handwrite something, it will usually be read, if it is legible.

Surprise someone with a handwritten letter that expresses interest in what the person does. Introduce yourself and offer to get to know the person better. Have a good, mutually beneficial reason to follow up on the letter.

If you cannot surprise someone you would like to meet, then send a letter to a supplier or vendor you have worked with, expressing your appreciation for the person's products and/or services. Invite the person to use your testimonial on a Web site. Ideally, the person will post it on a site and reference back to your site, increasing your organization's Web site traffic.

With this kind of challenge I have ended up on business book covers. People like to use testimonials to add credibility to their work. It is no accident that so many authors use testimonials on the jackets of their books, and by offering someone hand written recognition, you are creating a win-win scenario.

Buzzoodle Buzz Notes

List some people who might appreciate a surprise note.

To whom have you sent notes to for this challenge?

From whom have you gotten favorable responses?

Additional note area for actual benefits the organization has received due to your efforts on this challenge.

Buzzoodle Buzz Challenge #7

Any Day Card

> Difficulty..........................Simple
> Time.............................Quick
> Cost.............................Minimal
> Technology Required......None

Near the end of December you probably get all kinds of cards. Instead of doing what everyone else does, send some other types of cards that will stand out.

- Happy Spring.
- Merry June.
- Feliz February.

Take your pick, but pick something that will be a pleasant surprise and not a card in the stack. Feel free to send the regular holiday cards if you like, but unless you do something unusual, there is a good chance they will not create any buzz and may just end up tossed aside in a stack.

Thank you cards are another way to send someone a card. Send it for something that a person would not expect to get a card for. For example, you could send a thank you for being a good neighbor to another business close by. Consider sending a thank you card to someone who bought something from you a year ago. Thank the person for contributing to your current success and invite the person back in. There are a variety of options for the kind of cards you can write and send. Keep cards on hand along with postage so you can quickly dash off a card without interrupting your day.

Buzzoodle Buzz Notes

Make up some any day holidays and list them here.

To whom would you like to send cards?

How many cards have you sent to date?

From whom have you gotten favorable responses?

Additional notes for actual benefits the organization has received due to your efforts on this challenge.

Buzzoodle Buzz Challenge #8

Mail a News Clipping

     Difficulty.........................Simple
     Time...............................Quick
     Cost...............................Minimal
     Technology Required......None

Read a newspaper or magazine and find an article about a business or organization that interests you. Send a congratulatory note and the clipping to the business or organization that made the news.

In your note, include comments about why you like what you read and mention who you are, what you do, and what possible tie-in there is between the two organizations if there is any. You might invite the person to have lunch sometime.

Make sure the article is recent and be sure to address it to someone mentioned in the article, such as the CEO.

A variation of this might be a congratulations note for appearing on a talk show or the news, unless the person was in handcuffs. This is especially effective with start-ups and local businesses that are more likely to value one mention in the media and be more open to a connection to other people in the community.

News clippings are a common technique for salespeople to use in hopes of getting their name in front of people. What is not so common (therefore more buzz-worthy) is having non-salespeople send you the message. You might just surprise some people and make them take a second look.

Buzzoodle Buzz Notes

List some periodicals from which you could get interesting news.

How many notes/clippings have you sent to date for this challenge?

From whom have you gotten favorable responses?

Additional notes for actual benefits the organization has received due to your efforts on this challenge.

Buzzoodle Buzz Challenge #9

Social Networking

Difficulty........................Simple
Time.............................Ongoing
Cost.............................Minimal
Technology Required......Simple

Social Networking is a phenomenon that has occurred over the last few years on the Web. Social networking Web sites are Web sites that enable people to list information about themselves so they can network and meet people. There are many such sites, and it is not a bad thing to be signed up for multiple ones.

MySpace.com is one site that is very hot currently. It is more based on friendships and is a premier Web site, but it is not an easy place to create buzz unless young people are your target.

To find a list of more business networking sites, visit www.buzzoodle.com and look for the social network reviews.

Social networking sites work if you use them, but if you only sign up and forget about it, you will be unlikely to get any quality contacts. Make your profile as compelling as possible and be sure to connect with some people. Make a habit of using it a few times per month minimum and you will find that it will start paying off with valuable connections to new people and it will start expanding your network.

A few months after we started Buzzoodle we had several people in Fortune 100 companies and some venture capitalists contact us after finding me on these kinds of sites. It was a pleasant surprise.

Many of these sites also allow you to link back to your company Web site, which creates inroads to the company site and could help search engine ranking. The combination of links and a good buzz-worthy profile will get you steady interest from people surfing the social network.

Buzzoodle Buzz Notes

List social networking Web sites you have joined.

List the last date you logged in and interacted with someone through a social networking Web site.

Which people have you met because of this challenge?

List social networking efforts that have resulted in good buzz for the organization.

Additional notes for actual benefits the organization has received due to your efforts on this challenge.

Buzzoodle Buzz Challenge #10

Online Directory

> Difficulty..........................Simple
> Time................................Quick
> Cost................................Minimal
> Technology Required.......Simple

Online directories are profiles and professional listings in directories that can have a business use or can be for fun, as myspace.com is.

These sites have tools that can help you manage contacts in many cases and communicate with your broader network.

These directories can be another way to help new people find you, to create some buzz through a compelling profile, and a way to let people know when something about you changes.

We use Plaxo among other directories. When anything changes in a Plaxo profile, anyone else who is using Plaxo and has you listed as a Plaxo contact will be notified of the change. It is a great way to ping people on an occasional basis without being intrusive.

LinkedIn is another valuable tool that is part social networking and part online profile. LinkedIn helps you manage your network and, by going beyond your immediate contacts, it can be a powerful tool for growing your network, meeting new people, and creating buzz.

What makes a compelling, buzz-worthy profile?

Focus on telling people what makes you different from someone typical in your field. Also do not be shy about showing off your expertise. People are usually looking for experts, not novices. If you are not an expert yet, choose something you are passionate about and become an expert on that topic.

Buzzoodle Buzz Notes

In which directories are you listed?

With whom have you made connections via your online profile?

List people you have contacted after reading their profile.

Have you met people and gotten to know them well?

Additional notes for actual benefits the organization has received due to your efforts on this challenge.

Buzzoodle Buzz Challenge #11

Squidoo Expert Lens

Difficulty.........................Simple
Time.............................Quick - Medium
Cost.............................Minimal
Technology Required......Simple

Squidoo is a free service that allows you to build an expert lens (a single Web page on a specific topic). It is a portal you build with links and resources that create a portal to the subject. You can find it at www.squidoo.com.

A Squidoo Lens will drive more traffic to your organizational Web site, to your blog, and to articles and news that has been published about you and to anything else you want to promote. To see an example of what can be done with a Squidoo Lens, visit the Buzzoodle Squidoo Lens at www.squidoo.com/buzzoodle.

This site is easy to use even if you do not have any skills at building Web sites. If you do a good job of creating a lens people find useful or interesting, you will create a lot more traffic for your organization's Web site and you can establish yourself as an expert in a particular area.

You do not have to create a job-related lens. Some of the most interesting and popular lenses are centered on pop culture and personalities. Just be sure to at least mention where you work in your profile.

At the time of this writing, Squidoo is still undergoing minor changes and is moving the Google ad words around. Before you do a corporate lens, be sure to take a look at some other lenses and decide if it is the best option for you.

Buzzoodle Buzz Notes

List your lenses.

When was the last time you updated your lens?

Which lens masters have you contacted?

Which people have you gotten to know because of your lens?

List connections you have made due to the lens that have resulted in good buzz for the organization.

Buzzoodle Buzz Challenge #12

Tag Your Web site or Blog

Difficulty.........................Simple
Time...............................Quick - Ongoing
Cost...............................Minimal
Technology Required......Simple

Social bookmarks, or tagging, is a very common practice that helps people find your Web site, blog, or other online property. It also helps search engines properly index what you have tagged. Tagging tools are free, Web-based tools that you can use to build public bookmarks.

It works by creating a bookmark with text that describes the linked page. It also allows additional words (tags) to be associated with the link.

It is helpful if one person tags a page, but it is far more helpful if many people are tagging your page. Tagging builds more keywords associated with the webpage. More people bookmarking your page adds credibility to the page and more links to the resource to help it get found.

Take a few minutes and tag several Web pages from your organization's Web site with Del.icio.us [Just type that in your browser] or another social bookmarking site. It takes only a few moments to set up and periodically use. There are other sites out there as well, but this one is one of the originals and is very effective.

To make your bookmark more buzz-worthy, use a compelling, interesting tag and title. If people see it and bookmark it, it will continue to show up on the front page of your social bookmarking system and get more attention.

The long-term effect of the effort will be a higher level of Web buzz. Make bookmarking new pages a common habit.

Buzzoodle Buzz Notes

List where you have created social bookmarking accounts.

How many bookmarks are you tagging per month?

Have you noticed an increase in traffic to the Web site?

With whom have you shared your bookmarks?

Whom else do you know who has bookmarked a page from your Web site or blog?

Additional notes for actual benefits the organization has received due to your efforts on this challenge.

Buzzoodle Buzz Challenge #13

Blog/Message Board Comment

> Difficulty..........................Simple
> Time..............................Quick
> Cost..............................Minimal
> Technology Required......Simple

On the Web there are plenty of places to leave comments. Blogs usually have a place to make a comment, and so do message boards. Blogs usually give you the opportunity to link back to your organizational Web site, which will generate traffic and some buzz for your organization.

The better your comment and the more insightful it is, the more people will be curious about you and click over to your site. If your comment generates a discussion and gets people involved in the post or message board, it will generate even more buzz and clicks to your site or blog.

Usually, at the very least, a blogger will check out the site of someone who leaves a post. Choose a blog that is written by someone who interests you and you could make a very good connection.

When leaving a comment, do not write about something unrelated to the post, do not put in a bunch of links, do not promote yourself other than with a signature, and do not use the same comment on multiple blogs and message boards.

If you are unsure of how to find a blog, go to www.technorati.com and do a search on a topic that interests you.

Side Note: To start with, go to the Buzzoodle Blog and leave a comment about this book. Do an Amazon testimonial for this book as well and say something like "My name is Jack Smith and I work for big company. I found this book to be..." These are simple ways that we both benefit.

Buzzoodle Buzz Notes

List some blogs and message boards on which you have commented.

How many total comments have you left to date?

From whom have you gotten favorable responses?

Which people have you started interacting with regularly as a result of this challenge?

Additional notes for actual benefits the organization has received due to your efforts on this challenge.

Buzzoodle Buzz Challenge #14

Join/Participate in an Online Group

Difficulty..........................Simple
Time...............................Quick
Cost...............................Minimal
Technology Required......Simple

Joining an online group that interests you, has a lot of members, and is active is a great way to quickly reach a wide variety of people. You can join these groups in many places, but the most common are at the major search engines:

http://groups.yahoo.com
http://groups.msn.com
http://groups.google.com

Once you are a member, you can post questions and comments to the entire group. For example, you may have completed another Buzzoodle Buzz Challenge and written an article. You could ask the people in the group to critique it. This would be a great way to increase the effectiveness of another challenge.

Some of these groups are made up of people who are interested in business networking. These groups can be a powerful way to create buzz for your organization if you become an active member.

Pay attention to the rules and culture of the group. If you join and just start sending messages that are not a good fit, you may get a negative response.

Buzzoodle Buzz Notes

List some groups you have joined.

How many messages have you sent to the group to date?

From whom have you gotten favorable responses?

In which groups and people are you the most involved?

Additional notes for actual benefits the organization has received due to your efforts on this challenge.

Buzzoodle Buzz Challenge #15

Talk to a New Person in Person

Difficulty..........................Simple
Time................................Quick
Cost................................Minimal
Technology Required......None

What? Talk to a person in person? Yes, go out of your way to start a conversation with someone you might not have talked to had you not read this challenge. The elevator, if you work in an office building, is a great place to talk with someone. Or you could attend a networking event, talk to someone as you wait for your table for lunch or when you are at a convention or expo.

In order for it to be a Buzzoodle Buzz Challenge, it cannot be someone in your organization and it cannot be someone you would have talked with anyway. It has to be an extra effort. Ideally, you will ask what the person does and have the opportunity to talk briefly about your job.

The buzz happens because when people hear about your organization from multiple sources they are more likely to remember the organization and feel like they have a personal connection with it.

Here is a list of places I have recently met people: gym, kids' softball game, park, tour of another business, lunch, conference, and through a friend, just to name a few.

The big key for this challenge is to say "I am going to talk to someone new" and make it happen.

Buzzoodle Buzz Notes

List some people you have met with this challenge.

How many people have you kept in touch with whom you met?

From whom have you gotten favorable responses?

Where have you met people for this challenge?

Additional notes for actual benefits the organization has received due to your efforts on this challenge.

Buzzoodle Buzz Challenge #16

Contact a Reporter or Writer

Difficulty..........................Simple
Time...............................Quick - Medium
Cost..............................Minimal
Technology Required.......Simple

Writers and reporters get contacted all the time by people hoping to get some free publicity. That does not mean you should not try. The key is to provide them with something that will make them notice you.

Reporters will be more likely to respond to you if you offer them a scoop or can demonstrate some special knowledge of a subject that they may need in the future. Also, if you are a regular reader of reporters or writers, they are going to be more likely to take notice because they want to keep their readership happy.

The key with this challenge is to try to develop a relationship over a few contacts. Try to be helpful to the person you are contacting. Find out if there are any things they are working on that you could provide information for. Be careful not to contact them so frequently that they do not appreciate the effort. Take a longer approach and occasionally touch base with them, unless you have a particular issue that is timely and needs their attention.

I had the good fortune of being part of a story where I offered my expert opinion on Buzz Marketing as a sidebar to an article about someone else, all because the reporter remembered me. As a result, we got several calls from the exposure.

When the right stars align, a writer or reporter will be a very buzz-worthy contact. So keep trying with a variety of media professionals on a regular basis.

Buzzoodle Buzz Notes

List some media professionals you want to get to know.

When was the last time you contacted each one?

From whom have you gotten favorable responses?

List stories and buzz you have created with this challenge.

Buzzoodle Buzz Challenge #17

Contact an Old Employer/Employee

Difficulty..........................Simple
Time...............................Quick - Medium
Cost..............................Minimal
Technology Required......Simple

I often look back on all the people I have worked with in the last twenty years and wonder why I have not kept in better contact with those people. Just as I have advanced in my career, so have many of them.

Take a few minutes and look up an old coworker, boss, or employee. Get reacquainted and find out what the person is doing now. Talk about what you are doing. Find out if the person has any interesting news about anyone else you both worked with.

Over time, try to build up a list of people you worked with or went to school with. Keep it up to date with what they are doing now and e-mail them occasionally with a success story of yours. A great way to build this list is to go to your next class reunion or use your alumni association to find members you knew.

Many big companies are now creating alumni systems so they can stay in touch with employees who have moved on. They find this is a good source of buzz and it also helps them recruit new employees (or hire ex-employees back).

When doing this challenge, remember that buzz does not mean they are going to buy something from you or your company today. You are looking for people who will go out and say, "Never guess who I talked to..." and create a little word of mouth for you and the organization. If they become your customers it is icing on the cake.

Buzzoodle Buzz Notes

List people you have lost touch with and want to contact.

How many contacts for this challenge have you made to date?

From whom have you gotten favorable responses?

Has this challenge helped you get to know anyone better?

Additional notes for actual benefits the organization has received due to your efforts on this challenge.

Buzzoodle Buzz Challenge #18

Customer Follow-up

> Difficulty..........................Simple
> Time................................Quick
> Cost................................Minimal
> Technology Required......Simple

Simple and fast! Follow up with a customer and find out what the person likes about your organization. Is there something that the person thinks you can do better?

How you go about this challenge depends on the type of organization you are in. You should follow your organization's guidelines for this challenge. Some organizations will want to have formal questions, some may want to have one person do all follow-ups, and others will specifically not want to have staff members randomly calling customers.

If you do call a customer, do not treat it like a survey. Instead, just say you are following up with them to see how things are going and find out about the person's experience with the organization. Keep the call informal and friendly.

If a call is inconvenient, you can do a follow-up e-mail and ask a few open-ended questions. It is as important to let the customer know you are listening as it is to get valuable information.

In the event you get negative feedback, either resolve the issue or be sure to forward it to the appropriate person in the organization for follow-up. How your organization handles unhappy customers is a big factor in how much buzz you generate.

Buzzoodle Buzz Notes

List some customers with whom you can follow up.

How many customers have you contacted to this date?

What are some of the positive comments you have gotten from customers?

What are some of the negative comments you have gotten from customers?

Additional notes for actual benefits the organization has received due to your efforts on this challenge.

Buzzoodle Buzz Challenge #19

Call/E-mail a Person You Respect

Difficulty..........................Simple
Time................................Quick
Cost................................Minimal
Technology Required......Simple

Is there someone you would like to meet? It should be someone you respect who would be beneficial for you to get to know. In this challenge we suggest you stretch and think of someone who is not easy to meet, but not too difficult to reach either.

Contact this person and explain why you would like to meet. Briefly describe yourself and propose getting together for coffee or lunch. If there is any way that you can benefit the person, say so. If not, you could propose that the person act as a mentor to you in your career.

Some influential people enjoy acting as mentors to people who are working hard to grow and succeed. If you do want to ask them to act as a mentor, be sure to have a plan. You might have some goal setting with input from the mentor and meetings every three to four months to review progress. Find out if there is someone the person would like to meet or some other way you can help. Maybe you can help find someone for a position the person is having trouble filling.

I know several people who have famous mentors and they leverage the name and relationships to create more buzz for themselves and for their mentors in a big sort of way.

Buzzoodle Buzz Notes

List some people you would like to meet.

When was the last time you tried to contact a person you wanted to meet?

From whom have you gotten favorable responses?

Which people have you met and gotten to know?

Additional notes for actual benefits the organization has received due to your efforts on this challenge.

Buzzoodle Buzz Challenge #20

Mini Announcements

> Difficulty.........................Simple
> Time...............................Quick
> Cost...............................Minimal
> Technology Required......Simple

Post a mini announcement about your organization. Many newspapers, local newsletters, weekly papers, bulletins, chamber publications, and other publications will allow short announcements to be published. These are usually a few sentences maximum and they do not always have to be directly about your organization.

For example, you could say: "John Doe of XYZ Company wants to thank everyone at the chamber for helping 2006 be such a successful year. Contact me today if there is something I can do to make you more successful in the coming year."

This kind of message is not selling the organization as much as it is exemplifying the kind of employees an organization has.

If you cannot find a print outlet for your mini announcement, you can make a post to Craig's List (www.craigslist.com) that will take you a couple of minutes and it will generate traffic to the Web site. Craig's List is simple and I have heard of people getting incredible results from quick posts there.

To get the best effect, be creative and make these announcements interesting. If it just blends in with the other announcements it will get lost in the crowd.

Buzzoodle Buzz Notes

List interesting facts for which you could do mini announcements.

How many mini announcements have you sent to date for this challenge?

Where have you done mini announcements and on what date?

From whom have you gotten favorable responses?

Additional notes for actual benefits the organization has received due to your efforts on this challenge.

Buzzoodle Buzz Challenge #21

Digg Your Site

    Difficulty.........................Simple
    Time..............................Quick
    Cost..............................Minimal
    Technology Required......Simple

Digg is a site (www.digg.com) where people submit news and interesting Web sites to the community, and then the community votes on them. The vote is called a Digg, and the more people who digg your article, the more popular the article becomes.

The phrase "Digg Effect" has been coined to describe when buzz and Web site traffic from one post results in many visitors.

Digg is only one of several sites that have this kind of service. The new Netscape site has a service like this, and I have used others in the past. When using these kinds of services, be ready for some negative comments. Each post has messages threaded behind them and many of the cynical users will bash any post that does not meet their expectation. Some healthy debate is good, but be ready to ignore some of the comments you may get.

Special attention needs to be paid to the community of the site when you are using these services. If your post does not interest or conform to the community standards and culture, it will not get as favorable results and will be more likely to create bad buzz than good. You will get to know that culture only by participating some before you post your own stories.

If you are particularly interested in entrepreneurs and venture capital, go to the Go Big Network at www.gobignetwork.com and sign up for free to post links to your news and stories. The Go Big Network has a smaller group but it is very active and interesting at the time I am writing this. As always, check the Buzzoodle Web site for the most current information about these tools.

Buzzoodle Buzz Notes

List some interesting web resources you can digg or buzz about. Not the main homepage, but good articles or information that people will find useful.

How many stories have you posted on Digg or related sites?

Have you gotten favorable comments?

Additional notes for actual benefits the organization has received due to your efforts on this challenge.

Buzzoodle Buzz Challenge #22

Flickr Fun

Difficulty..........................Simple
Time...............................Medium
Cost...............................Minimal
Technology Required......Simple

Flickr is a Web site where you can post images and make comments. You can sign up for a free Flickr account at www.flickr.com. Buzz is created at Flickr by participating in the groups and uploading images.

Today it is more common than ever to capture and share images. Many people take digital photos at events they go to and post those to Flickr and on their blog.

By posting your image on Flickr and creating a blog post or Web page elsewhere that is associated with the image, you can get traffic from people who find you on Flickr. The critical part is to post a note with the image that has a link back to the blog post or Web site.

Flickr is just one more example of a great community that is sharing resources, information and helping people get to know you.

Flickr is also a good place to add images of a product, or maybe images of staff members, always linking to the main site so someone can get more details, of course.

At the time of this writing, Flickr is the most popular of these services. However, there are many services with similar features out there. Look around and find one you like. Remember, the goal is to upload images that will create some buzz and Web site traffic, not to find a place to store your family pictures. Do that from home.

Buzzoodle Buzz Notes

When did you open your Flickr or other photo sharing account?

How many images have you uploaded that are tagged and point to your organization or blog?

Have you gotten any favorable buzz from uploading the images?

Whom have you met because of this challenge?

Additional notes for actual benefits the organization has received due to your efforts on this challenge.

Buzzoodle Buzz Challenge #23

Personal Success E-mail List

Difficulty..........................Simple
Time...............................Ongoing
Cost...............................Minimal
Technology Required......Simple

There are people who care about you and your success. If there are not many, you can develop a group of people who act as mentors and advisors to expand your list. If they agree to help you with your career, they will be interested in hearing about your progress.

This challenge is an ongoing challenge where you develop this e-mail list and broadcast your occasional successes and progress to the group.

While this may seem self-serving, it is also a good opportunity to talk about the job, new things at work, and how the company is growing. Ideally, some of the people on your list who are following your success will get ideas for clients or contacts and help you grow your network, as well as help you have a big impact at work.

This is a less intrusive way to keep marketing your offerings or organization to family and friends. (A group that often does not appreciate directly being sold to.)

The occasional e-mail you send to this group should contain anything that could benefit both parties, such as job openings or discounts that are exceptional.

Since this is a group of people who care about your success, you may feel comfortable asking for help and advice. You can also say what you are looking for, such as wanting to meet someone with a particular skill set.

Buzzoodle Buzz Notes

List some people who would like to periodically hear about your success.

How many e-mails have you sent to this group to date for this challenge?

From whom have you gotten favorable responses?

Additional notes for actual benefits the organization has received due to your efforts on this challenge.

Buzzoodle Buzz Challenge #24

Did you Know? – Trivia

> Difficulty.........................Simple
> Time..............................Quick
> Cost..............................Minimal
> Technology Required......Simple

Did you know that Buzzoodle was started because Ron McDaniel of Liquid Learning got frustrated with members of his team not being willing to create buzz for the company because *it was not their job*?

Find interesting trivia points, about your company or otherwise, and use them to create more interest and thought about your organization. Every organization has interesting trivia about hurdles it has overcome or decisions that seemed small at the time but had a huge impact on the growth of the organization. Was the founder originally a horse breeder or a pilot?

These interesting trivia pieces are great to collect as a group and to insert into e-mails, invoices, e-mail signatures, and other communications to liven up an otherwise boring document. If you use good, interesting trivia in this way, people might actually look forward to your invoice. I know it is a long shot.

Good trivia can make a great conversation piece if someone asks about the organization as well. By having all team members know interesting trivia points, they will be able to talk better about the organization.

Make a point of collecting interesting organizational trivia and making it a part of your communications. It will help build advocacy from people outside the organization who will have interesting things to repeat about you.

Buzzoodle Buzz Notes

List interesting trivia and facts about your organization.

Where have you published the trivia facts?

Additional notes for actual benefits the organization has received due to your efforts on this challenge.

Buzzoodle Buzz Challenge #25

Instant Messaging

Difficulty........................Simple
Time...............................Quick
Cost...............................Minimal
Technology Required......Simple

One common form of communication today is instant messaging. There are many instant messaging tools available, including Yahoo Instant Messenger and MSN. Instant messaging works by popping up a chat with the person you pick from your list and having a live, back-and-forth text dialogue.

Newer versions of instant messaging have video and other features available as well.

For this challenge, use instant messaging to communicate some interesting news or buzz about your organization to someone on your list. Get a group of people who are interested in news about how you are doing and feed the interest via live messages.

If you have a group of people to whom you have quick, personal access, then you have a group that can become advocates for you and your organization. Instant messaging is just one way to communicate with them regularly, quickly, and in a very personal manner.

A word of warning: Instant messaging can be very disruptive to your day at work. Many workplaces have banned it because anyone can contact you anytime and chat. If you use instant messaging, keep it set on a "do not disturb" setting when you are trying to get work done.

Buzzoodle Buzz Notes

List some people you instant message.

What kinds of things do you buzz about through instant messaging?

From whom have you gotten favorable responses?

Has any instant messaging effort resulted in good buzz for the organization?

Additional notes for actual benefits the organization has received due to your efforts on this challenge.

Buzzoodle Buzz Challenge #26

Text Messaging

Difficulty..........................Simple
Time................................Quick
Cost................................Minimal
Technology Required......Simple

All the kids are doing it! Text messaging is like instant messaging, but on the cell phone. You can send a quick note to someone's cell phone from your phone or from some Internet sites.

What makes text messaging special is that it usually reaches people wherever they are. This also means you have to use it with some care because the people you message may be paying per message and you are also interrupting them with your message, so do not send blatant advertisements or any other message that will just annoy them. As a rule of thumb, if they care about the message, or if it makes them smile, it is worth sending. Most people will pay a nickel for a smile.

For this challenge, text message a quick note to someone who is not in your organization but does know you and will like to hear from you. If the recipient is not texting all day long, he or she will appreciate the alternative form of communication. Consider inviting the person to lunch or getting together sometime soon. If it is someone you know well, text message the next big success you have to let the person know about it.

We often text message successes among each other here at Buzzoodle. If I am in a meeting and I get a text message, I glance at the phone and smile. Usually the person I am meeting with asks if I need to get it, and I can say "We just got a big sale…" or something like that and continue with the meeting. It does create buzz and can generate some interest and discussion.

Buzzoodle Buzz Notes

List some people you can text message with confidence.

How many times have you sent a message to date for this challenge?

From whom have you gotten favorable responses?

Which text messages have resulted in good buzz for the organization? What were they about?

Buzzoodle Buzz Challenge #27

E-mail a Useful Link to Someone

Difficulty.........................Simple
Time...............................Quick
Cost...............................Minimal
Technology Required......Simple

This is one of those challenges that seem so simple, yet you may not be doing it often enough. If you read news and information on the Internet, you probably see things all the time that other people you know might appreciate. Make a habit of e-mailing links and a quick note to people who might find something useful or interesting.

If you have a good signature for your e-mail, you are creating good buzz for your organization just by being helpful. We all know that good customer service is a huge part of having a successful organization, but what about beyond customer service? What about just being helpful, friendly, and a great resource for people you know? This is how you take customer service to the street, figuratively speaking.

This challenge is an easy example of the Buzzoodle philosophy of creating buzz and great relationships through helping people. It will keep you top of mind, make people look forward to hearing from you, and generate more referrals for you and your organization.

Imagine how great it would be if you heard someone say, "Those people over at XYZ Company are so helpful." A group effort doing things like this challenge can make it happen faster than you think.

Buzzoodle Buzz Notes

List some people, along with their interests, to whom you can regularly send news.

How many e-mails have you sent to date for this challenge?

List what buzz results this challenge has generated for the organization.

Buzzoodle Buzz Challenge #28

Testimonials

Difficulty.........................Simple
Time...............................Quick - Medium
Cost..............................Minimal
Technology Required.......Simple

The cultivation of testimonials is a good way to create buzz with the person you are asking and to help create more success stories for you to use in other situations. It is important to get people who have used your services or bought your products to take a moment and think about the benefits they have received. Once they put it into words, they are better able to know what to say when they recommend you.

Ideally, your organization will have a way to capture testimonials from clients and keep them in a database. If customers give you permission, using them on your Web site is a great way to get more search engine hits, add credibility to the organization, and give something back to the people who are doing the testimonials, by way of a link to their Web site.

Even if there is not an organizational effort to cultivate and record testimonials, it is a good way for you to collect feedback and endorsements for the job you are doing and to develop buzz-worthy stories you can spread.

Begin this challenge by checking with your buzz organizer as to how the organization solicits testimonials and where to publish them. If you are in charge of it, create a questionnaire for soliciting testimonials and feedback, and set a goal to get a certain number each month.

Buzzoodle Buzz Notes

List some people you could ask for testimonials.

Who have you gotten testimonials from so far?

What is the best testimonial you have gotten to date?

Have any of your requests resulted in buzz for the organization?

Additional notes for actual benefits the organization has received due to your efforts on this challenge.

Buzzoodle Buzz Challenge #29

Celebrate Success

Difficulty..........................Simple
Time...............................Ongoing
Cost...............................Minimal
Technology Required......Simple

How do you get more people to create more buzz? Celebrate success and let people know when you get buzz-worthy results.

There are many tools that can be used to celebrate your successes as an organization. If no one in the organization has set up a formal way to disseminate success yet, mention it to management. It is critical that an organization knows what successes it is achieving and what stories it can tell.

The tools to tell the stories depend on what works best for the organization. A simple bulletin board can work if some people do not have computers. Also a company newsletter or reading the items at a staff meeting works well.

If you have a technical workplace and everyone has access to the Internet, you can use your intranet to post stories. If that is not available, consider starting an online group, setting up a wiki or a workplace blog to let people know about your success stories.

One of my clients has been using an eNewsletter for years. The software archives the article on the Web as well as sending it via e-mail. The archives now get more hits than the main Web site, even though it is published only for employees. Of course, the public reading about success and how the organization treats the employees is a good thing too.

Celebrate success every day in a public way.

Buzzoodle Buzz Notes

What is the last buzz you created and celebrated with others?

What have been your biggest buzz successes to date?

What are the best buzz successes you have heard about other people?

Buzzoodle Buzz Challenge #30

Write a Blog

Difficulty........................Medium
Time..............................Ongoing
Cost..............................Varies
Technology Required......Simple

One of the top ways to create buzz on the Web is to have members of an organization write blogs. Blog is short for Web logs and it is just a term for a Web site that is updated frequently and is organized in reverse sequential order.

There are many places you can start a blog. Free options exist like Blogger.com. If you are serious about blogging and want to do corporate blogs, Buzzoodle provides professional blog packages. It is important to choose your blog provider carefully because it is not easy to change later, and free blogs are not always seen as credible. While blogging technology is simple, there are many customizations and additions possible. Be sure you can grow with your blog.

For this challenge, set up a blog and keep posting to it. By regularly posting to a blog at least several times a week, you can expect to increase search engine traffic, and if you write on an interesting topic, you can expect to build an audience over time.

Well-written blogs can create a huge amount of buzz. Entire books are written on buzz marketing with blogs.

Many large companies are requiring their staff to blog. Be sure to keep your posts professional. Assume your boss will find it someday, even if you do not tell the boss you are doing it.

If you are writing directly on a topic relevant to your industry, be sure to link your blog to your organization's Web site. Your blog must have the duel goal of creating buzz for the organization and establishing you as an expert in your field.

Buzzoodle Buzz Notes

When and where did you set up your blog?

How many posts do you plan to post each week? Are you meeting this goal?

List when you post comments and track backs to your blog on other blogs.

Who have you met via blogging?

What good buzz has happened because of your blog?

Buzzoodle Buzz Challenge #31

Have a "Get to Know You" Meal

Difficulty.........................Medium
Time...............................Medium
Cost...............................Varies
Technology Required......None

Have a lunch or dinner with someone you know slightly. Spend the time finding out about each other and ways you can help each other succeed. A coworker does not count. It should be someone you have met in your industry.

One great way to do this challenge is to get an advance list of people who are going to be at a convention or expo that you are planning to attend. First Google them and find out a bit about them and their company. Then send them an e-mail or call them and find out a bit more about them and invite them to have lunch or dinner around the conference.

This is just one creative way that you can expand your network and create some buzz for your organization through a planned meal.

Be sure to listen more than you speak, and try to find connections that you can make for them. For example, someone may mention writing a book and you may know a publisher. Making that connection will make you more of a valuable resource to the person, make the publisher happy, and give both a reason to think of you as a well-connected person who is important to them.

Getting to know people and trying to help them be successful is one of the best ways to build your network and create a little buzz for you and your organization.

Buzzoodle Buzz Notes

List some people you would like to get to know better and why.

How many people have you met and gotten to know better?

Whom have you gotten to know well because of this challenge?

What buzz has this challenge created for you and the organization?

Buzzoodle Buzz Challenge #32

Host a Dinner Party

Difficulty..........................Medium
Time..............................Medium
Cost..............................Varies
Technology Required......None

Host a dinner party at your house or in a restaurant that has a private room for large groups. Invite a variety of people from your network who may not have met each other but could benefit from meeting. Also, find out if they would each like to bring a guest who might benefit from meeting others in the group.

Instead of having them all tell what they do, you may ask them to have a success story from the last couple of months to tell. This way, you will be able to tell your success story as well.

Some very successful people have used dinner parties to build their network and their business. Hosting an exclusive party each month for a few new people to get to know the rest of the group is a great way to strengthen existing relationships and expand your circle of influence. As host, people will appreciate your effort to connect people and if they get value from attending, they will anxiously look forward to the next one.

This could even be an organizational effort, sponsored by the company, and involving partners, employees, clients, and prospective clients. Find ways to interact and connect people, and people will be buzzing about you.

Buzzoodle Buzz Notes

List some people you would like to invite to a dinner party.

How many group dinners have you had and how many people came?

What great connections have you gained from this challenge?

What buzz for the organization has happened because of this challenge?

Buzzoodle Buzz Challenge #33

Arrange a Networking Lunch

Difficulty..........................Medium
Time...............................Medium
Cost...............................Varies
Technology Required......None

Helping other people succeed is a great way to create buzz and get people talking about you and your organization. For this challenge, arrange a networking lunch. A networking lunch is when you invite two to three other people to lunch with you who do not know each other. Ideally each of these people will benefit and enjoy meeting the others for the first time.

One technique is to invite someone to lunch and when you talk, ask who the person would like to meet. Then call that person and invite him or her to lunch. Explain that you are having lunch with the other person and that person has always wanted to meet this person. This will make it easier to arrange.

Care is needed on this challenge that no one person attending is just out to sell things to the others. If that happens, you may just interrupt the effort by saying "This lunch is just for getting to know each other. You can follow up later."

There have been salespeople in the past that have used this technique to build very successful careers and they did not even push their products or services; they were just building good will.

To create more buzz, you could ask them to describe the most exciting thing that has happened in their organization in the last three months. Have your buzz story prepared for your turn.

Buzzoodle Buzz Notes

List some groups of people who do not know each other but may like to meet.

List dates and attendees of your network luncheons.

Additional notes for actual benefits the organization has received due to your efforts on this challenge.

Buzzoodle Buzz Challenge #34

Publish an Article

Difficulty..........................Medium
Time...............................Medium
Cost...............................Minimal
Technology Required......None

A few years ago, it was challenging to get an article published. Now, there are many Web sites hungry for content and happy to link back to your organization's site in exchange for a well-written, interesting article.

This challenge requires that you publish an article, and it is easier than you think.

If you have the resources and connections to get published in a print magazine or newspaper, that is a great route. If you are not accustomed to publishing and do not have any connections to help you get published yet, go to one of the many article repositories on the Web.

Be sure you get credit for any article you publish and get a link back to your Web site in the signature of the article. Links to your organization's Web site from a variety of quality sites will increase the search engine ranking and make it more likely people will find you.

If you search for article repositories on the Internet there are many options. Make sure one has been around for a while and that it prominently displays author information and the articles in the presentation of the articles on the Web site.

If you are already blogging, it is fairly easy to repurpose a good blog post into a more formal article. Reusing your content to create more resources will get you more exposure and buzz.

Buzzoodle Buzz Notes

List some topics you can write about that people will be interested in reading.

How many articles have you published for this challenge?

Have you been contacted by anyone because of an article you wrote?

Additional notes for actual benefits the organization has received due to your efforts on this challenge.

Buzzoodle Buzz Challenge #35

Meet More Neighbors

Difficulty.........................Medium
Time................................Medium
Cost................................Minimal
Technology Required......None

Chances are, you live in a neighborhood of people with similar demographics as you. In fact, the neighborhood you live in and the house you live in are major contributors to your profile.

So what better way to build your network and create some buzz than by getting out and meeting more people like yourself? Many of your neighbors have similar jobs as you and similar interests. Having them know you and understand who you are and what you do means they will think of you when they need something you or your organization can provide.

So how do you meet more neighbors? Being involved in things your kids are involved in is one way to build a network. Even if you do not have kids, consider the times when people are out and approachable as an opportunity to meet a new neighbor.

If they are out walking and so are you, it is easy to start talking. What about a garage sale? They are just waiting for you to come up and start talking, and maybe buy their old coffee table.

I find it easy to get people to ask what I do. If I meet new people, I say, "I own a business and work all the time, so I have not met many people around here yet." The next question is what do I do, without fail. I quickly tell them what I do and then start asking them about what they do. People like to talk more than listen, and I look for opportunities to make a referral or follow-up later.

Buzzoodle Buzz Notes

How many of your neighbors, within a two-block radius, do you know?

How many new neighbors have you met due to this challenge?

Which new connections are valuable as a business connection?

List meetings that have resulted in good buzz for the organization.

Buzzoodle Buzz Challenge #36

Send a Press Release

Difficulty	Medium
Time	Medium
Cost	Minimal
Technology Required	Simple

Press releases used to be the domain of PR specialists, but not anymore. Now there are many press release Web sites where you can upload a news item for free.

For this challenge, write up some news. Unless you are in charge of the company's news and press releases, do not send out any corporate news without getting it approved. Instead you can write up some relevant news about you and send it out through one of the many free news outlets, like www.prweb.com.

If you want to get more bang for the press release, these services also provide paid listings that get wider exposure.

Copy the style of a press release and write it in a way that will not conflict with your organization's official releases. For example, you could say, "Ron McDaniel, CEO of Buzzoodle, will be teaching two seminars at the university this fall on buzz marketing...." It is personal news but paints the organization in a positive light. The link and the information will create more buzz and better search engine results for your organization.

If you are unsure of the policies of the organization, you will want to check with the PR or marketing department before publishing any press releases. We also recommend all organizations have Buzz Standards and Guidelines in place to help guide the team in these challenges.

Buzzoodle Buzz Notes

List some press release ideas.

How many press releases have you submitted and where?

Which press releases have generated the most buzz or traffic?

Additional notes for actual benefits the organization has received due to your efforts on this challenge.

Buzzoodle Buzz Challenge #37

Give a Speech

Difficulty..........................Medium
Time................................Medium
Cost................................Minimal
Technology Required......None

Not everyone loves to give speeches, but it is a very valuable skill to work on. If you are not accustomed to giving speeches, join a local Toastmasters club or other speaking club and get some practice and valuable pointers. You will have a captive audience there to start building buzz with.

If you are already comfortable with speaking, look for an opportunity to give a speech in the community. There are many opportunities, such as at a Rotary Club, a chamber, a university or school, a networking meeting, or a conference. Set a goal to start speaking and let people know you are interested in speaking engagements. Opportunities will start to present themselves.

Associations usually have opportunities for members to speak at conferences and meetings as well.

Even if you speak on a topic not related to your job, you can introduce yourself and mention your title and where you work. The key with successful speeches is that you are giving people something of value, you have good energy, and you make them think. If you can do that, you will find that one speech will lead to more, and your reputation will grow. You may move from doing free speeches to paid speeches, from short presentations to keynote speeches, and from unknown to national expert.

If members of an organization are out doing speeches on a regular basis, it will create a lot of buzz for the organization as a whole.

Buzzoodle Buzz Notes

On what subjects could you develop a thirty-minute speech?

Where can you get an opportunity to speak?

Where have you done speeches related to this challenge?

What buzz or opportunities have been created by the speeches??

Buzzoodle Buzz Challenge #38

Volunteer

Difficulty..........................Medium
Time................................Ongoing
Cost................................Minimal
Technology Required......None

Volunteering is a very rewarding way to create buzz. Some people volunteer on a regular basis and others only occasionally. It is a good way to meet people and to engage people in conversation about what they do while working toward a common cause.

It could be working with kids or the homeless, mentoring business students, teaching a language to nonnative speakers, or taking any other opportunity to work with people and talk to more people. Keep in mind that the people you are helping may not spread buzz about you but other volunteers or the organizers will.

If you are a busy business owner and cannot make time for this, you can always sponsor a Little League team or sponsor some other event. It does not get your story out their as personally, but it is still a way to show you are contributing to the community.

Another great way to volunteer and meet people, as well as create some buzz, is to help with an event. Helping staff a booth or organizing an event, such as a marathon will result in meeting many people and is usually a one-time commitment. I have also found that helping on issues of economic development have helped me connect with some great people and created considerable buzz for us.

There are a lot of ways to create some buzz through volunteering. Find something you will like doing and get involved.

Buzzoodle Buzz Notes

What are some potential volunteer opportunities you can pursue?

What things have you volunteered for because of this challenge?

Have you been able to create any buzz for the organization while volunteering?

Buzzoodle Buzz Challenge #39

Online Interview/Podcast

Difficulty.........................Medium
Time.............................Medium
Cost.............................Minimal
Technology Required......Simple - Medium

Podcasts are a new hot content type on the Web. They are basically sound files that are posted to the Web and can be downloaded to devices and listened to in the car, from a portable device or on a computer.

Many podcast business sites are hungry for content. Do an Internet search and find a site that does podcasts related to your industry and offer to do a telephone interview with them.

A podcast interview will be around for years and continue to create a buzz about you and your organization for as long as people find the topic interesting enough to download and listen to. Most podcast publishers will also publish text and links along with the podcast, which will generate traffic back to your Web site or blog.

If you want even more buzz from podcasts, learn to make them yourself and interview others in your industry. It is a great, low-cost way to become a leading expert in your field.

You can create a podcast from a speech, a staff meeting, a roundtable discussion, a training session, or a one-to-one interview. See the more advanced podcast challenge in this book for more details.

If you are going to do podcast interviews frequently and have a consistent theme, post links to your podcast in podcast directories and you will get traffic and buzz.

Buzzoodle Buzz Notes

What audio recording opportunities would make good podcasts?

What could you do an interview about with authority?

Who is doing podcast interviews on that subject?

How many podcast interviews have you done?

List podcasts that have resulted in good buzz for the organization.

Buzzoodle Buzz Challenge #40

Conduct a Survey

Difficulty.........................Medium
Time..............................Medium
Cost..............................Minimal
Technology Required......Simple

Many companies do surveys – customer service surveys, customer satisfaction surveys, etc. Asking people to answer a few short questions is a good way to collect valuable information and create some buzz. For example, if I asked you a few survey questions as follows, I would be less interested in your responses and more interested in what thinking about the questions did toward your understanding of Buzzoodle.

Sample Survey Questions:
*   Are you aware that Buzzoodle can provide complete Internet marketing services?
*   Has your organization ever had staff buzz training, such as what Buzzoodle provides?
*   What discount would make a bulk purchase of this book for all of your staff an easy decision?

You can see that asking a few questions of people you come in contact with or as a follow-up to a sale can increase knowledge and interest in your products and services. Whether you are doing a formal survey or just asking questions, be prepared with the kind of questions that will educate and create interest.

Buzzoodle Buzz Notes

What are some questions that would actually educate someone on a product or service?

What valuable answers have you collected via questions and surveys for this challenge?

From whom have you gotten favorable responses?

List questions that have resulted in good buzz for the organization.

Buzzoodle Buzz Challenge #41

Local Government Involvement

Difficulty..........................Medium
Time................................Ongoing
Cost................................Minimal
Technology Required......None

You would be amazed at how getting involved in local government can create buzz for you. This is especially easy to do when you are not in one of the big metropolitan areas.

Our company has been located for years in a smaller community that has easy access to some larger cities. Our city has been great in working to keep us in the city. The city buys products and services from us and creates buzz about us. All because of one e-mail I sent to the economic development coordinator.

Now the city manager buzzes about us and the city staff buzzes about us. We get invited to speak at the university, we win awards, and are constantly cited as proof that the city is on the right track. We help the city use us as an example of the city's success. It creates buzz for them and for us.

You can begin to get to know the city officials via e-mail and letters, and by going to public meetings or city council meetings. People there are usually happy to talk with residents and are very approachable. Just keep in mind that they are busy and it will usually take more than one contact to make a favorable impression.

One thing I always make sure of is that the city economic development team always knows our success stories. Our success is the city's success, and city officials talk about us in speeches, in the paper, and with other resident business owners.

Buzzoodle Buzz Notes

What city officials would you like to meet?

Do they have blogs or newsletters that will help you get to know them?

Whom have you met and how often do you keep in touch?

Additional notes for actual benefits the organization has received due to your efforts on this challenge.

Buzzoodle Buzz Challenge #42

Open House

Difficulty..........................Medium
Time...............................Long
Cost...............................Varies
Technology Required......None

Get people through the door and interacting with you. This challenge is better done as a group and with the proper approval, as your boss may frown on an unexpected group of people showing up for a tour and snacks.

There are many excuses to have an open house. Customer appreciation, grand opening, new product release, summer fun, or winter warm up are just some ideas.

Don't do an open house for the sake of an open house. Have a goal and some buzz to create. You could have the open house to unveil something buzz-worthy. People do not come to an open house just because there are cookies. These are people who are at least curious about you and are all potential advocates who will carry your message, so be ready to impress them, give them a story to repeat, and show them a good time.

The hardest aspect of having an open house is getting people to come. Give yourself plenty of time to get the word out and build some excitement.

Another variation of this challenge is to allow another organization to use your offices for a party or reception. I recently attended an event for a soccer association that ended back at an after-party in wonderful offices of a software company. It was a good time and increased my knowledge of that company a great deal.

Buzzoodle Buzz Notes

What are some of your ideas for an open house or tour?

What people do you know who would be willing to come?

What do you want to achieve with the open house?

Additional notes for actual benefits the organization has received due to your efforts on this challenge.

Buzzoodle Buzz Challenge #43

Interview a Leader

Difficulty..........................Medium
Time.............................Medium
Cost.............................Minimal
Technology Required......Simple - Medium

This is a great way to create some buzz, meet someone influential and build your network. Interview a leader in your industry or someone who interests you.

Your interview could be via e-mail or phone. It could be published in a company newsletter, Web site, blog, or podcast. The key is that you get to meet someone, find out more about the person and use that information to publish content that creates some buzz for you and for the person you are interviewing.

If your own executive team seems unreachable, consider doing an interview with them and then letting the staff know what is interesting about them. This will arm everyone with additional buzz collateral.

Be sure to follow up with the person to say where it was published or posted and what people are saying. The person may even publicly link to it if it is on the Web, giving you more credibility and buzz.

Want even more buzz? Try doing an interview a week in a blog. That would be fifty plus people you would interview and also your readers would contact you. This technique can bring in many connections and create a lot of buzz for you and your organization.

Buzzoodle Buzz Notes

List some people you would like to interview.

How many interviews have you conducted?

How and where did you publish them?

Additional notes for actual benefits the organization has received due to your efforts on this challenge.

Buzzoodle Buzz Challenge #44

YouTube.com

Difficulty..........................Medium
Time.............................Medium
Cost.............................Minimal
Technology Required......Advanced

Youtube.com is a Web site where you can post video. It is free and has a true community around video. You can make comments, watch other videos, tag your own video, and publicize the video via other avenues to increase its popularity.

For example, I posted a video we had an intern do about Buzz at http://www.youtube.com. It did not get a huge response, but it is important that if you search on Buzzoodle, you get a video made by Buzzoodle. If you do not do this, then you are leaving the rest of the world open to create videos about you.

If you do not have the expertise to create a video yourself, you can usually find an intern, student, or neighbor's kid who would love the experience. You can then repurpose the file for your Web site, youtube.com and other video casting options. Consider using YouTube to post videos of testimonials, success stories and any other positive video message you can get. If one catches on in the community it will create a lot of interest.

At the time of this writing, YouTube.com is the most popular. However, keep an eye on www.Buzzoodle.com to see if other technologies are emerging for creating more buzz.

Buzzoodle Buzz Notes

What videos can you make that can be posted on the Web?

How many have you posted?

Have you gotten any buzz from the post?

Who have you met because of your video?

Buzzoodle Buzz Challenge #45

Meet Business Neighbors

Difficulty..........................Simple
Time................................Quick
Cost................................Minimal
Technology Required......None

Chances are real, live people work in some of the businesses around where you work. Proximity is a great excuse to meet someone new, and it could lead to some serious buzz.

Several years ago we had a power outage. I stopped in at another office in our complex and asked if they were having the same trouble. We got to talking and they have been great clients of ours ever since. We sometimes get their payroll if no one is going to be around and we let each other know when good networking events are coming up.

For this challenge simply stop into a business that is close by, even if it does not seem like an exact fit. Take a few moments to introduce yourself and find out what they do.

If it is a good fit for your organization, invite your new friends to visit your place as well.

If you want to take this challenge to the next level, consider organizing a business block party. You will have a great excuse to meet people in other businesses close by and you will become well known and talked about in the immediate area.

Buzzoodle Buzz Notes

Which nearby businesses have you visited?

From whom have you gotten favorable responses?

What good buzz has this challenge created for your organization?

Additional notes for actual benefits the organization has received due to your efforts on this challenge.

Buzzoodle Buzz Challenge #46

eNewsletter or Newsletter

Difficulty..........................Medium
Time................................Ongoing
Cost.................................Varied
Technology Required......Simple

There are a lot of options for you to create a newsletter and distribute it to people who are interested. There are also many of reasons you would benefit from doing this.

Newsletters, either via e-mail or print, will keep you fresh in the minds of the people receiving them. I have seen salespeople put together very simple eNewsletters that contain just a business tip of the week. This keeps their relationships going and keeps them in front of the people they want to do business with. It can also create buzz if your eNewsletter has great content and gets forwarded to others.

Newsletters are also an effective way to communicate success stories to your company's team members so they can buzz more. By creating an internal eNewsletter that focuses on celebrating success, you will be more effective in getting everyone to increase visibility.

For this challenge, identify your target audience, identify topics that will interest the audience and explore tools for creating your newsletter. It may be as simple as a copy machine initially or an e-mail list and your e-mail software. Eventually you will want to go to an eNewsletter service, such as Outstanda, to create online resource centers and news. The advantage of these kinds of services is that they simplify everything and have great list management features. It is also nice to see how many e-mails are opened, what is being read, etc.

Buzzoodle Buzz Notes

What is your topic and audience?

How many subscribers do you have?

List dates you have published a newsletter.

From whom have you gotten favorable responses?

When has this challenge resulted in good buzz for the organization?

Buzzoodle Buzz Challenge #47

Produce an eBook

Difficulty.........................Medium
Time...............................Medium
Cost...............................Minimal
Technology Required......Simple

For this challenge, create an eBook. An eBook is a book that can be downloaded online, usually in PDF format.

The advantage of an eBook is that it can be e-mailed and will act as a salesperson for you if done correctly. The key to a successful eBook is to make it well branded. Your organization should be prominently featured so that people benefit from the free information yet are likely to contact you for more information.

An eBook sounds big, but many eBooks are simply Power Point slides that read like a book. Often it is just an article marked up in an easy-to-use electronic format. What may only be ten or fifteen pages can be spread out into bullet points, graphs, and images to fill a fifty-page eBook.

You can eventually develop it into a comprehensive eBook that you can sell or offer as a free incentive to sign up for your eNewsletter or as a free item with purchase.

If your eBook provides value to the reader, you will find that it is being e-mailed around to people you have never met, and it will create considerable buzz for you and your organization.

Buzzoodle Buzz Notes

List topics you can write about that can make an interesting eBook.

What eBooks have you created?

From whom have you gotten favorable responses?

Additional notes for actual benefits the organization has received due to your efforts on this challenge.

Buzzoodle Buzz Challenge #48

Nominate an Organization

Difficulty.........................Medium
Time..............................Medium
Cost..............................Minimal
Technology Required......None

In print and on the Web, there are many opportunities to nominate organizations for an award. Some of them are free and some of them cost money, but winning some of these can be the difference between a stagnant company and huge buzz. For this challenge you must nominate someone.

Not only is it a good idea to nominate your own organization for an award, it is also an excellent idea to nominate your clients or sponsors. Whether they win or not, they will most likely find out you nominated them and they will feel appreciated. They will mention to other people that you nominated them as well, so it is a great way to get other organizations buzzing about yours.

If the organization cannot be nominated, sometimes you can nominate the organization's leader for special recognition. That might be a good way to get a raise as well, as long as it is not for the worst boss of the year award.

You can usually find opportunities to nominate the organization just by searching for the word "nominate," the current year, and area or industry. You can also keep an eye on marketing sites and blogs to find out about nomination opportunities.

Marketingsherpa.com often publishes opportunities to nominate people or businesses for awards and I list them on the Buzzoodle Web site when I come across them.

Buzzoodle Buzz Notes

List opportunities for nominating someone. Also list the month they are due by, because many will repeat next year.

Whom have you nominated and for what?

What buzz has your nomination created?

Buzzoodle Buzz Challenge #49

Challenge a Coworker to a Buzz-Off

Difficulty..........................Medium
Time.............................Medium
Cost..............................Varied
Technology Required......Simple

This challenge is less about doing one challenge and more about motivating several people to create more buzz. Get a group of people with similar interest and attitude about buzz and have a buzz-off. Find someone to act as the impartial judge. They will review the various buzz efforts and results, and will award a winner based on specific criteria and on a specific date, as agreed upon.

This is a great way to jump-start some buzz creation and get people involved in the organization. You could even form several teams instead of individual groups.

It is always nice to give awards to the person or group that wins. We suggest a large trophy and a parade honoring the winners in downtown Cheyenne.

In the event that you do not want a parade and trophy you cannot carry, consider creating a friendly competition between you and someone else and regularly comparing buzz efforts. You could even create separate blogs and compete to see who can build up traffic the fastest.

If you are in a very small business, you can meet someone working in another similar-sized business and get together and compare buzz efforts. You can even help each other, if you are not competitors. Spreading stories about someone else is sometimes easier than spreading them about your own organization.

Buzzoodle Buzz Notes

Whom will you compete against in a buzz-off? What is the start and end date?

List each buzz challenge completed during your buzz-off and the results.

Buzzoodle Buzz Challenge #50

Podcast Show

> Difficulty..........................Advanced
> Time...............................Ongoing
> Cost...............................Varied
> Technology Required......Medium

Podcasts are sound files put up on the Web that can be downloaded into devices to be listened to, usually via a feed. Audiences can subscribe to the feed so they get the latest materials.

Creating a regular podcast that goes out to your audience is a great way to create buzz, but it does take some effort. Much like a blog, it is important to keep at it and have a clear topic so people want to come back.

Podcasts can be created quickly on sites like Odeo.com or you may want to purchase software to better mix and publish the podcast.

For this challenge, learn how to do a podcast and start producing a podcast show that is published at least once a month. Before you begin, listen to professional podcasts that are similar to the topic you are going to cover. Pay close attention to what makes them seem professional and explore if you can do that for yourself.

Also make a list of people you would like to interview and topics you would like to cover. This challenge is going to take some planning and you will most likely see results only if you stick with it for a while.

This is one of those challenges that might be easier if you get a group of people to participate. Find someone in the organization who likes to assemble the podcast, another person who wants to be the voice, and another who wants to promote it, and you will on your way to big buzz success.

For more information on podcasting, visit Buzzoodle at www.buzzoodle.com.

Buzzoodle Buzz Notes

What podcast topics can you develop?

How many have you posted?

Have you gotten any buzz from the post?

Whom have you met because of your podcasts?

Buzzoodle Buzz Challenge #51

Host a Seminar or Training Session

    Difficulty.........................Advanced
    Time...............................Long
    Cost...............................Varied
    Technology Required......Simple

Put together a training session or seminar. This could be job related or it could be something that is of interest to you. For example, if you work with computers you may want to teach people basic computer use at the local library. No doubt you will have the opportunity to say something like. "At XYZ Company, where I work, we use Microsoft, but you may have a Mac at home."

Just like that, you have mentioned where you work, have established that the organization has employees who are experts who train others, and have shown a level of caring above and beyond another company that may not be doing training sessions.

Some of these people will not remember your name, but they will say, "That nice young woman from XYZ Company taught me a lot." Depending on the seminar, you may be able to have very candid conversations and mention the kinds of people you are trying to meet.

Even better is to do a more comprehensive seminar that attracts the kind of people you want to meet in the first place, and establishes you as an expert in your field and as someone they all want to know.

By doing these kinds of events regularly, you can build up a reputation and buzz over time.

Buzzoodle Buzz Notes

On what topics can you do a seminar or training session?

What places may be interested in having you teach?

Who is likely to attend your seminar?

Which seminars have you conducted, when and where?

Buzzoodle Buzz Challenge #52

Unexpected Booth

> Difficulty..........................Advanced
> Time.............................Medium
> Cost.............................Varied
> Technology Required......None

There are many different places where you can put up a booth and gain valuable exposure as well as meet new people. With this challenge, think about an opportunity to put up a booth in a place that is less expected.

A booth is always more than just a booth. The booth and the people at the booth are selling the organization and creating interest. Do not think just about the people walking by, but also the people in the other booths. I treat the other booths as an important part of the conference and treat them as a primary target.

So what are some examples of unexpected booths? How about your company doing a resume evaluation at a career fair? How about passing out water or kids' paint sets in an "art in the park" event? Could your organization benefit from a booth that teaches people at a trade show how to blog?

By setting up a friendly, interesting booth that does not blend in with the obvious booths at the show, you are more likely to get noticed and create more connections with the people attending, as well as the people in the other booths. Have a couple of people staff the booth and get out from behind the booth to meet people, and you will have a successful time creating some buzz.

Buzzoodle Buzz Notes

What kind of booth could you set up?

What creative/different kinds of events could you get a booth at?

List booths you have helped staff. Place, date and effectiveness.

Buzzoodle Buzz Challenge #53

Organize a Group

Difficulty.........................Advanced
Time................................Ongoing
Cost................................Varied
Technology Required......None

This challenge requires that you organize a group of some sort. There are many options to choose from and it does not have to relate directly to your job, although you will get more buzz for your organization if you start a group that is in your field. The group should meet regularly and have some structure and a clear purpose. It should also be fun and useful for the people who attend.

You can form a Mastermind Group for business owners, a SIG (Special Interest Group) for people in your field, a networking group, a dog enthusiasts group, a good parenting group, a Spanish club, or anything else that interests you and will at least interest a few other people. If appropriate, consider doing the event in your office or conference room. Your organization may be willing to sponsor the event or you can charge a fee for people to attend, to cover your costs.

Be sure you can create some buzz at every meeting. Maybe each person stands up and does an introduction and lets people know what kinds of things he or she is looking for. Hone your message to make it memorable and buzz-worthy. Focus on success stories and people will remember you better.

One story I heard from Brian Stark of the Stark Group of Companies is how he started a local investors group that eventually led to millions of dollars of business and 50% of his total business revenue. Not all through one big deal but through a network of people who started referring him. He is now the largest private lender in the region.

If you simply do not have time to start an organization, join one and get involved.

Buzzoodle Buzz Notes

What organization did you start or join?

How often do you have or go to meetings?

What topics do you cover?

What buzz have you created because of the group?

Buzzoodle Buzz Challenge #54

Become a Board Member

Difficulty..........................Advanced
Time...............................Ongoing
Cost...............................Minimal
Technology Required.......None

Many local nonprofit organizations have a board of directors. These boards are usually made up of volunteer board members who help guide the organization.

It is not always easy to get on a board, but once there, the group you are working with will probably be made up of very influential and well-networked people. I met someone once who had a spouse join these boards because they were networking with the spouses of some of the most influential business people in the region. The person found it very effective for building a personal network and the spouse enjoyed being involved with the community.

To get on a board, you need to become involved with the organization very actively for a while beforehand. When you are seen as someone that is committed to the cause, you will have more influence in the group and can ask for the opportunity to sit on the board. It may also just be offered to you.

Whether you do it yourself or encourage a spouse, target some boards that have influential people whom you would like to meet as members. Find out what it takes to get on the board and work at it over time. It is best if it is an organization you care about as well.

The long-term buzz effect of working with boards of directors can be exceptional. It is one of the more difficult challenges listed and will take time and effort to achieve. Start identifying interests and opportunities today and work toward getting on a board.

Buzzoodle Buzz Notes

List some interests you have and organizations that are good fits with that interest.

Do they have a board of directors? Do you know anyone on the board?

To which boards or executive committees do you belong?

What buzz have you gotten from being involved?

Buzzoodle Buzz Challenge #55

Conduct a Focus Group/Roundtable

Difficulty...........................Advanced
Time................................Medium
Cost................................Varies
Technology Required.......None

I recently sat on a technology roundtable to help a college assess the effectiveness of its tech curriculum. College officials did a great job of getting me to the campus. They took time to educate me on their mission, introducing me to the other great people participating, and fed me breakfast.

The end result? I loved driving an hour to give them free advice. I later hired some people from their program.

Your challenge is to conduct a roundtable or focus group for your organization. The information you are collecting will be valuable, but also remember that the experience the participants have is the key to creating buzz.

Members of this group could be giving you feedback on a new product or service, they could be assessing your customer service, or they could be beta users of software you are developing. There are plenty of reasons to ask people for feedback, and if you make the experience memorable, they will carry your message out to the public and create some buzz on your behalf.

If conducting a formal focus group is not something you can do in your position, start asking people for feedback and testimonials as you work with them. This still gives them a feeling of being listened to and appreciated, which is key for getting customers to create buzz for you.

Buzzoodle Buzz Notes

What topics would you like to cover in a focus group?

Whom would you like to invite to participate in a focus group?

When have you conducted focus groups and where?

What valuable information did you get back from the group?

What buzz came from conducting these focus groups?

Buzzoodle Buzz Challenge #56

Conduct a Customer Contest

Difficulty..........................Advanced
Time...............................Ongoing
Cost...............................Varies
Technology Required......Simple

Customers who care about you are more powerful than your internal marketing department. You just need to enable them to communicate with you.

This challenge is to design a customer contest that gets great feedback from customers and gets the customers involved with the organization. For example, a contest could be to write the best blog post that exemplifies what your organization has done to help the customer. Wow, all those people saying nice things about you at the same time might make you explode. Watch out. If you don't want to do blogs consider a less technical approach, such as a simple bulletin board clients can use to post testimonials.

Another idea is a homemade video showing a creative use for a product. See the Buzzoodle Challenge about youtube.com to see how easy this would be to conduct.

Be sure to let the participants know that you reserve the right to use their media in your own promotions. Think about how powerful a group of video testimonials would be on the Web.

Another ongoing contest could be people who snap a picture in a public place of someone using your product. I have seen authors highlight these kinds of things on their blogs.

These kinds of customer-created advertisements have credibility and sincerity that is hard for a marketing team to achieve. Use this challenge to create buzz in a big way.

Buzzoodle Buzz Notes

What do you want from your customers? Video? Blog posts? Testimonials? Referrals?

What is your contest and what can someone win?

What are the most buzz-worthy outcomes of your contests?

Buzzoodle Buzz Challenge #57

Organize a Charitable Event

Difficulty..........................Advanced
Time...............................Medium
Cost...............................Varied
Technology Required......Simple

Do not underestimate the value of this challenge for creating buzz. If your organization does a charitable event, you will get a variety of different buzz opportunities while doing a good deed at the same time. It is hard to beat that.

For this challenge, organize an event that will increase exposure and income for an important charitable organization. Plan it in such a way that you will have the opportunity to contact other businesses and ask for participation. This will give you a valuable reason to make contact without directly selling your product or service. Make sure you clearly identify yourself and where you work, and explain that you are involved in the charitable event.

Then do the same to generate interest in the event. Getting people to come to the event will take contacting people in different ways and getting the attendance where you want it. Many people will come if the event has some value to them while at the same time helping the charity. Do not underestimate the importance of this.

I recently went to a free breakfast for a charity, and then gave a donation because I figured the breakfast and networking alone were worth that. Ernst & Young had sponsored the breakfast, so we all won and the charity made money.

Organizing a charitable event in hopes of building some buzz for you is not unethical. It is a win-win scenario that can create a lot of buzz and expand your network if done with care and a real focus on helping the charity.

Buzzoodle Buzz Notes

About what charitable organizations do you care the most?

What do they need and what can you do to help?

What events have you organized to help a charity?

What buzz did you gain from helping the charities?

Part Five

Your Buzz Strategy

Now that you have read all of the buzz challenges, do not put the book away in a dark drawer. As obvious as some of these challenges may seem to you, you will not keep them all in mind all of the time. The next time you find yourself with more than five minutes to kill or you just need a fun break from a tedious project, pull out this book and do one of the simple challenges.

Be sure to write in it as well. Writing in it will help you remember things you have done in the past for challenges. I recommend that your organization have all employees keep a copy of this book on their desk so team members can browse other people's buzz books to see what they have done. This helps the team keep buzz top of mind. It also helps promote group collaboration on buzz and provides a nice self-policing technique. Instead of managers asking people about buzz creation, employees with a blank book on the desktop will feel self-conscious until they have some buzz success to write about.

Creating buzz is fun. The number one problem this book is likely to create is that people will find creating buzz is so much fun, they may not prioritize their day properly. Remember that one of the most important things for creating buzz and word of mouth is great, buzz-worthy products and customer service that goes beyond what people are expecting. This should never suffer because you are blogging or taking people to lunch.

If you are in a management position, be sure to understand the goals, policies, and preferred challenges of the organization and communicate those to the rest of the staff. If you are a staff member, remember to check with a manager before ever publishing or communicating a message if you are not sure the subject is acceptable.

Buzzoodle Buzz Marketing is about getting everyone involved in creating more success for the organization and more buzz for the individuals in the organization as well. By using good common sense and setting clear goals, as an organization you are preparing to achieve exceptional growth, visibility, and success.

Getting every person involved in creating buzz is the cornerstone of having a great team and a buzz-worthy organization.

Measuring Your Buzz Results

One of the most difficult aspects of word of mouth and buzz marketing is measuring the results. It is fairly easy to track the results of an ad in a newspaper or the number of clicks on an Internet advertisement, but it is difficult to measure the ROI (Return on Investment) for a Buzzoodle Buzz Marketing effort.

The first, most obvious answer is that if your sales or donations go up, it must be working. Does that mean if your sales do not go up that it is not working? No. It means you may need more time to build a critical level of buzz.

I do not like that answer though. It is possible to get a good estimate of your buzz effort. The unfortunate piece is that there is not an individual number, beyond sales, that can tell you if it is working or not. It is in fact many metrics. Below is a list of some of the key metrics you can measure that will help you estimate your success in creating buzz and word of mouth.

Buzz Creation

An obvious thing that can be measured is to have team members record when they create buzz. This does not have to be a high-priced custom system. Simply use one of the free resources online to create surveys and make a short form that staff can go to and record each buzz effort. You could ask them name, date, Buzzoodle Buzz Challenge #, link (if applicable), and short summary.

This will let you know who is making an effort and see if your focus on buzz marketing is paying off.

Blog Mention

One of the most common ways that marketers measure word of mouth today is by measuring the times you are mentioned on blogs. You can easily see who is talking about you by visiting technorati.com or blogsearch.google.com and doing a search on your name. If your organization has a blog you can register it at Technorati and watch its ranking numbers as well. These numbers represent the number of people that have linked to you.

Web site Traffic

If you are doing a good job of creating buzz, your Web site traffic should be increasing. Don't look only at the general traffic numbers. Also look at where your traffic is coming from via referral links. If you see an increase in sites linking to you, your buzz marketing is working.

Media Appearances

Be sure to record whenever your company is mentioned in the newspapers, magazines, on TV or in other forms of media. If members of your team are serious about creating buzz, many of them will start to get noticed by these media organizations and it will increase interest in the organization.

Employee Satisfaction Survey

If your work environment is a place where everyone feels like part of a winning team that is helping the organization succeed, you will see positive employee satisfaction results in a workplace survey.

Customer Satisfaction Survey

If you do regular customer satisfaction surveys, you should notice an increase in the satisfaction from customers. Buzz efforts should be getting employees to follow up with them more frequently. Plus, if customers are hearing positive buzz about their vendor, they will have a more positive feeling toward them.

The "I have heard of you" effect

You may not be measuring this one directly, but shortly after starting our Buzz Marketing effort more and more people started telling me "I have heard of you..." Many of these people were surprised we were even in Ohio as they thought we were some big agency on one of the coasts. You will know your buzz marketing effort is working when you keep hearing people say they have heard of you before, even though it is the first time you are meeting them.

Call/Inquiry Volume

You may not have much of a Web site to speak of if you are a local restaurant or some other business that does not do much online marketing. Even so, you can measure the number of calls in a day you get and see if the volume of calls or people stopping in has increased over time.

Contacts Quantity

If you have an organizational-wide CRM (Customer Relationship Management) system or online contact list, you can see how quickly the number of connections is increasing. If your team is out creating more relationships and is good at keeping this kind of system up to date, you will see an increasing number of people listed.

How Did You Hear About Us?

Hopefully you always ask this question of new clients. You may find you are getting more responses like: "I am not sure." "Several places." "My cousin Judy is married to Bill who works with John's wife and said I had to talk to you. I think John works for you." – Confusing, I know, but that is the world of word of mouth and buzz.

The biggest factor of success will be if a majority of the team keeps creating some buzz on an ongoing basis. It is not a question of if this strategy will work, but if your team will be able to keep at it, keep their enthusiasm up and offer great products and services. Measure those metrics and use them to reward star team members and your organization is making a good investment and heading in the right direction.

Are You Ready for Buzz?

One thing that is often overlooked is doing an assessment of your products and services before creating buzz. If you have a Web site that currently never generates leads or sales, what good is it if you double the traffic? None. More people kicking the tires of your product will not help if your tires are flat.

Review your products and services. Are people happy with them? Is your customer service exceptional? Does every part of your organization exude excellence? If not, do not create too much buzz too fast or you may end up with bad word of mouth.

Some recent research I recently read suggested that minor feature enhancements and usability improvements did more to create word of mouth than anything else. What that means for you, having just read this book, is that you may very well have wasted your time if you do not have a high-quality product or service. You can trick some people to try a less than remarkable product, but you cannot trick them to get all their friends to try it too.

Beyond the products and services themselves, does your Web site have clear conversion goals, such as an invitation to contact you that they cannot miss? Is your marketing material high quality? Do you make it easy for people to contact you and does your image inspire them to step outside of their comfort zone and connect with you?

If you are having trouble in these areas, have someone familiar with marketing, especially Internet marketing and word of mouth marketing, evaluate your products, services and Web site and look for ways to improve them.

Buzz Resources

Every day changes occur, especially with that Internet thing involved. What is hot and buzz-worthy this year may be outdated or even not in use next year. For that reason, this book has been written with some examples but not with comprehensive resources that name many technologies. For that, please visit **www.Buzzoodle.com**.

There you will find articles, blogs, Web pages, a Buzz directory and links to other valuable resources. To stay up to date on all buzz topics, I advise you to subscribe to the eMagazine. We will be continuously adding and evaluating new opportunities and tools that can help you create buzz.

And don't stop with reading the Web resources. One of the biggest obstacles for creating buzz is a fear of reaching out and connecting with people. If you visit our site or my blog, make sure you leave a comment or send me a note saying hi. I want to hear from people. I want to know what you like and do not like about what we are saying, and get great buzz stories and anecdotes to use in future books.

A great bonus buzz challenge is to get mentioned in other people's books and articles, and it is easier than you think. We landed in a race horse breeding magazine just from some simple buzz efforts. Send me a good story that illustrates a buzz challenge and I may use it in the future or post it on our Web site to illustrate a point.

About the Author

Ron McDaniel is an author, speaker, trainer, and founder of several successful start-up companies. He developed his own version of Buzz Marketing because of his own frustration at getting everyone in the company to be excited about the product and services and willing to look for opportunities on their own time to create some buzz.

Ron still works with clients of Outstanda and Buzzoodle that want to create a comprehensive marketing strategy. Buzzoodle and Outstanda help organizations take control of their future and develop a buzz and Internet marketing strategy that they can maintain and that uses their own staff and resources.

Outside of the business, Ron is a father and enjoys being very involved with his child's education and development. So much so that he helped his daughter Alexandra start and run Kids Roar when she was eight years old. (www.kidsroar.biz) Kids Roar is a business that is run exclusively by kids for kids. It is a vehicle for Alexandra to achieve financial independence and be able to buy her own horse. She might just learn something too.

Freely contact Ron via e-mail at ron@buzzoodle.com

Glossary

Marketing Terms

Advocate

Any person who advocates the use of a product or service without direct compensation to create the message.

Buzz Marketing

A marketing strategy to create elevated levels of word of mouth through events that cause a buzz. Extraordinary news items, celebrities, shocking information, and other techniques can all be used to increase the word of mouth for a time.

Stealth Marketing

The unethical practice of deceiving people into believing you are genuinely creating word of mouth when it is actually a paid effort. Often creates bad buzz if you get caught.

Viral Marketing

A marketing technique whereby the message or product has a strong likelihood of passing from person to person and spreading with no impetus from marketers after its release.

Word-of-Mouth Marketing

A marketing strategy to enhance and elevate positive word of mouth among consumers and create a stronger base of advocates for the organization.

Buzz Technology Terms

Blog

A blog is short for Web log and is a Web site with regular entries that are posted in reverse chronological order. The technology for maintaining a blog is usually very simple.

eBook

An electronic book, often in PDF format, that can be e-mailed or downloaded from the Web.

eNewsletter

An electronic newsletter that reaches readers by e-mail and may also reside on a Web site in archives. Systems exist to make eNewsletters easy to build, publish, and manage.

Expert Lens

Lenses are one-page Web sites that pull together all the valuable resources on a particular topic. The site www.Squidoo.com hosts lenses currently.

Instant Messaging

This is the act of instantly communicating with someone else, usually via the Internet. Free tools exist to make this easy and can be found with a simple Web search on instant messaging services.

Podcast

This is the method of publishing audio files to the Web and through syndication so that they may be listened to on portable devices and computers.

Social Networking

Online social networks are groups of people who communicate regularly via technology. Social networks self-form in often free sites that facilitate group activities and communication.

Text Messaging

Text messaging is the act of sending a text message to someone who has a portable device, usually a cell phone.

Vodcasting

This is the term for the video version of podcasting. Vodcasting is when you make video on demand available through syndication services.

Buzzoodle Buzz Marketing

Bulk Book Discounts

Discounts for bulk orders start at ten copies. Place bulk orders directly with the author by visiting www.buzzoodle.com or contacting him at ron@buzzoodle.com.

Online Buzzoodle Courses

Buzzoodle offers online courses on the web. Courses include:

- It's Part of your Job - Buzz Marketing for New Hires
- Buzz Marketing refresher course
- Various, industry-specific buzz marketing courses.

Buzz Marketing Speaking and Training

Ron McDaniel is available to speak at your next event or conduct a Buzzoodle Buzz Marketing training session with your organization.

For more information or to reserve a time, contact ron@buzzoodle.com